MW00623696

BE
a note
WHO
that changed my life
YOU
& the secrets
# CAME
that will change yours too.
TO BE

BE
a note
WHO
that changed my life
YOU
& the secrets
CAME
that will change yours too.
TO BE

TARA RENZE

Be Who You Came To Be: *A Note That Changed My Life & The Secrets That Will Change Yours Too,* copyright © 2020 by Tara Renze. All rights reserved including the right of reproduction in whole or in part in any form, except for brief quotations in printed reviews, without prior permission of the publisher. Direct requests to tara@tararenze.com.

ISBN: 978-1-7374220-1-3

First printing 2021

Printed in the United States of America

Book Cover + Book Design Layout by
Sarah O'Neal | *eve custom artwork*

*For More Information &
to purchase the book please visit
TaraRenze.com*

The note that changed my life. It was written to my newborn son by my eighty-seven-year-old grandmother.

September 2007

Dear Benjamin,

Having pictures of you is such a joy! You are such a beautiful baby. For 9 months I've spent hours imagining in my mind how handsome you would be, but even in my dreams I just didn't succeed. You are one of a kind and will continue to awe us all with expressions of your love, your mind, sensitivities, and creativity.

Be who you came to be. Love will guide you.

—Dot

dedication

This book is dedicated to YOU and the woman you came to be.

My Grandmother left this note for Ben. In my heart of hearts, I believe she left it for me to share with you. My wish is that this book brings you closer to the woman you were predestined to be.

You are perfectly flawed. You are beautiful. You are loved. You are enough.

Shine your authentic light and be who you came to be.
Love will guide you.

xoxo-Tara

secrets

I saw the angel in the marble, and I

carved until I set him free.

MICHELANGELO

intro

I wrote a book; yes, this book. It only took half my life to write it. I'm officially an author.

I started thinking about becoming an author when I was in my 20s, even though I didn't have a clue what I would write a book about. I wasn't an "expert" on anything then, and I'm not an "expert" now. I've written this book from my heart, based on truths and lessons I've learned in my life; It's my passion, purpose, and mission to help others "Be who they came to be."

Before we begin, let's take a step back to the stories behind the books that never got written and the story behind this story.

Not long after graduation, I married my college sweetheart, Scott. We were both determined to start successful careers. He studied chemical engineering while I pursued a communications degree; he went to work for an Engineering firm, and I was one of those "odd balls" who graduated from college and said, "I want to be in sales!" After multiple offers for mediocre sales jobs, I applied for a job I was incredibly underqualified for but seemed like the perfect job for me. I figured, "What the hell!" and faxed in my resume (yes, this was still the age of the fax machine). No kidding, I got the job!

This was my first lesson in the real world: **never play small.** Even if you're "underqualified," you can make up for it with tenacity, hustle, attitude, and work ethic. The job was as a "National Marketing Director" for a publishing company—we produced marketing brochures for high-end, custom home builders. I traveled the country meeting with builders and closing deals. It was invigorating, fun, and a great way to get my feet wet in the sales world.

Like many sales professionals, I hopped around a bit before finding my dream sales job. Who knew that my dream job was with an online job board. But it was, and I LOVED it. It was the early 2000's and job boards ruled the employment space. I started in sales and worked my way up to leadership. I led and managed two sales offices before I facilitated their national sales training program.

Not only did I love this job, but I also loved the company and the culture. Sales and leadership was my passion. I loved the entire sales process—from that first cold call to the million-dollar close. It was fast, high profile, fun, and incredibly fulfilling. And I was good at it. So naturally, in my 20s, I tossed around the idea of writing a book about how to be successful as a young professional in sales and sales leadership. I even had a book idea centered around "Mistakes I made as a young sales professional, so you don't have to."

In my 30s, my husband Scott and I started our family. Ben was born when I was thirty, and Jack was born when I was thirty-two. I will be sharing more about becoming a mom; Ben and Jack are definitely my most significant accomplishments in life, but having children changed me and my career path. I no longer wanted to be hustling million-dollar deals, managing salespeople, and traveling two to three days a week; I wanted to be home and present with my children.

So. . . I made a big change. I left the corporate world and shifted my career to a home-based business. Never in a million years did I think I'd climb the corporate ladder to leave it all behind to work from home, but

I did. And it was the perfect "fit" for my life; I could still flex my sales and leadership muscles while being at home with my boys.

During my 30s, I outlined a book celebrating Moms and encouraging new traditions. For instance, on a baby's first birthday, celebrate the mom, not the child. Instead of bringing gifts for the baby, bring gifts for the mom. The entire party is to pamper, nurture and celebrate the mom and her baby. Yes, of course, the baby would still get to eat its first piece of cake, but let's face it, it's not like the child even remembers their first birthday. It's the MOM who is worthy of a party. If you've had a child, you know that the mom is most deserving of gifts and praise when her child turns a year old.

That book never got written . . . but I still think the "1st Birthday" idea is pure gold.

I'm in my 40s now, and I was destined to write this book, *Be Who You Came to Be*. For years I pondered a note my grandmother left for my son before she died: "Be who you came to be," she wrote, "Love will guide you."

She had the gift of beautiful penmanship and spent hours every week writing letters to family and friends. Most of her notes were just catching us up on her life—what she was reading, what was for dinner that week, what her rose garden looked like, what our ornery grandfather was up to, and always an update on her dog, Cookie, and two cats, Love and Chris.

But the final note she penned for my son was different. It was a heartfelt letter of love written by an eighty-seven-year-old woman to her great-grandson. She put on paper her thoughts on his authenticities, what he might be like, and the man he would grow up to be. The last two sentences of this note she signed, *"Be Who You Came to Be. Love Will Guide You."*

Such a simple yet profound piece of advice; I've thought about it every day since. I've thought about this advice not just for my boys but for me. "Who did *I* come to be?"

And so here I am at age forty-four—a wife, mother, entrepreneur, keynote speaker, and author of my first book.

In addition to the social media platforms on which I share daily, I've spent the last four years as a keynote speaker for various companies, conferences, and organizations. One of the things I'm constantly asked by speaking bureaus and women who attend my events is, "Do you have a book?" Until NOW, I would say, "Not yet, but it's in the works!"

The truth is, I've written and rewritten this book a hundred times. But for some reason, I just couldn't get it right.

I consider myself a lifelong learner. Strong business acumen is something I've always prided myself on. And I joke that nothing will make you more intriguing at a cocktail party than being well-read. (That's a fact. I've been testing that theory for half of my life.)

If you spent an afternoon in my office, you could thumb through the business books that line the shelves. On these shelves, you'll find an array of sales and leadership books from unknown authors to well-known business advisors and 21st-century thought leaders.

For years, I envisioned my own book on that shelf, a book that might land on the business book section of your bookshelves (or in your Kindle library). But for some reason, I just couldn't get it done. I couldn't write the "business" book. The business-book format wasn't really my style, and with each chapter I wrote, I felt pangs of imposter syndrome.

Then, an epiphany.

I couldn't complete the book because the book wasn't a reflection of the AUTHENTIC ME. I realized I didn't really want a business book after all. Both my true north and innate desire guided me to write and publish a book that looks just like the one you're reading now: hard cover, gold foil, pretty fonts, quotes to remember, small chapters to read leisurely and ponder for days, lots of stories and a pretty enough book that you'd leave it on your coffee table and gift one to your best friend.

> *That was ME. That is me. And this is my book.*
> *This is the author I came to be.*

The manuscript I spent twenty years trying to write was finished in about six months.

It has been said that our perception is our reality. I had this insane notion that to be taken seriously as a speaker and emotional intelligence practitioner, I needed a business book. Once I freed myself of this insidious lie, the writing and process started flowing. The words appeared on paper, and the pages came to life.

One of the many truths I discovered while walking through this journey of becoming an author is that too often, we find it necessary to live in a world created by other people, with all of the expectations and demands they put on us. While living in community with expectations and responsibilities can be helpful, it can also cause us to wither away if we associate our identity with other people's lists of do's-and-don'ts.

One "aha" I hope you have while reading this book is that you have to stop trying to fit into "containers." Instead, you must create your own "container," soil, and space to live the life you desire. Be who YOU came to be and create the life you've always dreamed of.

So, thank you for reading my book—my authentic, non-traditional business book.

Do me a favor—snap and post a pic of yourself with the book (maybe sitting near your coffee table or desk) and tag me on Instagram. I want to see your beautiful faces and the spaces the book is spending time in.

This book is your OFFICIAL permission slip to
BE WHO YOU CAME TO BE.

I know, it's easier said than done. Putting our authentic self into the world can seem intimidating, scary, and perhaps even impossible. But trust me, the world is waiting for you to be who you came to be.

The ideas, perspectives, lessons, and advice you'll get from this book have been tested, lived, and compiled my entire life. I share ONLY what I know as a truth, what I love, and what has worked for me.

My wish is that in the time you read or even skim this book, you will get closer to the authentic version of you. Give yourself PERMISSION to show up as the authentic, perfectly flawed, beautiful YOU. The world is waiting for you to shine your bold light.

My favorite coffee mug has the Michelangelo quote on it: *"I saw the angel in the marble, and I carved until I set him free."*

Let's start carving away at who you came to be.

PART

one

CREATE IT

Life isn't about finding yourself.

Life is about creating yourself.

GEORGE BERNARD SHAW

THE HAPPINESS QUEST

You only live once, but if you do it

right, once is enough.

MAE WEST

THE HAPPINESS QUEST

I spent most of my 30s attempting to manufacture happiness. A mentor told me, "If you want to be successful, you need to be happy." So off I went to create HAPPY. I wanted to make my kids happy, colleagues happy, family happy, and husband happy. But what I found was that my desire to create happiness for everyone else left me feeling tired, exhausted, and quite frankly . . . not happy.

The worst part about desiring happiness is that the more you chase it, the further it can get away from you.

And let's be realistic; we are HUMANS. We aren't smiling and static emojis. We aren't meant to be "happy" all of the time.

If you research "happiness," you'll find lots of different definitions and opinions on what "happiness" is. Happiness is often defined as a pleasant *emotional* state that is characterized by feelings of contentment, joy, gratification, satisfaction, and well-being.

During the 1970s, psychologist Paul Eckman identified six basic emotions he suggested were experienced in all human cultures: happiness, sadness, disgust, fear, surprise, and anger. And on top of the basic six emotions, there are more complex and combined emotions—yes, you might rightfully recall Pixar's *Inside Out.*

But it doesn't take a movie reference for you to know and agree that we experience a multitude of emotions every day. Reflect on the last twenty-four hours. What are ALL of the emotions you have felt? If we were in Vegas (yes, I love Vegas), I'd bet $100 you would have experienced much more than just "happiness."

So why is it we constantly seek happiness?

One of the primary reasons we are consistently seeking happiness is because we are constantly being told to be "BE HAPPY." You can't pick up your smartphone without being reminded to:

Be Happy.
Choose Happy.
Get Happy.
Live Happy.
Don't worry . . . be Happy.

Books, t-shirts, bumper stickers, commercials, and advertisements are reminding us that we should LIVE HAPPY. The happy list never ends.

In my work as a speaker, author, and influencer, I have the good fortune of talking with a lot of women. They all have different stories, motivations, career paths, family lives, and authenticities. I love learning about their lives, family, career, passions, and what makes them tick. I'm always curious to find out what fulfills them. What are their goals, aspirations, and talents? Most of all, I love asking them this question, "What do you want in your life?" And most of the time I get this answer: "I just want to be happy."

I get it. I hear you. I've desired it too. I don't think I know one person who doesn't love the FEELING of being happy.

But the truth is, it's not a realistic or achievable life goal. It is impossible to manufacture happiness. Trust me, I know because I've tried. And yes, I've tried to "choose" happiness. You can't just "choose" happiness either.

I consider myself a realistically optimistic person and wake up every morning feeling hopeful for a great day, but there are so many big and small things that can dramatically shift your overall emotion or mood. Ever spilled a cup of coffee all over yourself? It's hard to "choose" feeling happy when something as trivial as this happens. So when the big life stuff happens, it's even more unrealistic to "choose happiness."

As much as you'd like to be happy all the time, you can't think *happiness* into existence. The reason we desire happiness is because we have the capacity to feel, which creates the compulsion to avoid many other emotions—sadness hurts; fear makes us feel small.

To truly experience happiness, you have to give yourself space and freedom to feel lots of other things. We understand what

HERE'S A SECRET

Abandon your happiness quest; focus on what makes you feel fulfilled.

———

sadness, anxiety, fear, and dismay *feel* like. And this is why we desire those epic moments of happiness and success.

Guess what? I've discovered the secret to creating genuine happiness and unlocking higher levels of success in life. Are you ready? Here it is:

Abandon your happiness quest; focus on what makes you feel **fulfilled.**

Happiness is the *end* result of our actions, relationships, and things in life that bring FULFILLMENT. Yes, the secret to genuine happiness is to focus on what is FULFILLING in your life.

NOT EASY, BUT WORTH IT

This is my philosophy on all life,

not just when it comes to love. All

the best things are terrifying, but

that's why they're the best things.

Nothing worth having comes easy.

You have to be afraid to want it,

afraid to lose it, afraid to try. If

you feel that, then you know you're

on to a winner.

THOMAS S. MONSON

NOT EASY, BUT WORTH IT

Take a minute and think about the most fulfilling things in your life.

Who are your most fulfilling relationships with?
What is the most fulfilling work you've done?

For many, the most fulfilling relationships are those with their family. My family provides the deepest level of fulfillment I've ever experienced.

I grew up with two older brothers, who are still two of my best friends. We have three cousins who are also some of my favorite people on the planet. I've always been incredibly close with my parents and had the good fortune of knowing and loving both sets of my grandparents. And my mom is the girlfriend I'm most excited to share big news with and the first person I call every morning.

But of course, the MOST fulfilling relationships I've ever had are with my husband, Scott, and my two boys, Ben and Jack. Creating a family of our own has been such a rewarding journey. Scott and I have been married for over twenty years, and that alone is incredibly fulfilling. And if you're a mom, you know there is no love more fulfilling than the love we have for our children. Being a mom is the most fulfilling love I have ever experienced.

In addition, I find immense fulfillment in my friendships and relationships outside of family.

And, my work has always been deeply fulfilling to me. From my career in sales to social selling to coaching other women, my work has fulfilled me in profound ways. And of course, authoring this book has been one of the most fulfilling things I've ever done.

After taking your fulfillment inventory, you'll realize that fulfilling relationships and work are what create EPIC moments of happiness and success; this is what delivers our happiest moments.

And while you take those fulfilling things into account, consider that fulfillment created through any of those relationships or endeavors does not come easy. In fact, they are usually the HARDEST things we do in life.

Family is not easy.

Marriage is not easy.

Raising children is not easy.

Work is not easy.

Relationships are not easy.

Writing a book is not easy.

_____ is not easy.

Fulfilling work and relationships require discipline, grit, determination, tenacity, courage, patience, forgiveness, and love.

Yet while this quest for fulfillment is not always easy, it's always worth it as it creates genuine happiness.

So let's keep digging into fulfillment. The following Secrets in Part One are an extension of defining fulfillment. Not only is it the secret to epic happiness and success—it is a *mindset* you can start enacting today.

THE

CHERRY

ON TOP

The greatest happiness you can

have is knowing that you do not

necessarily require happiness.

WILLIAM SAROYAN

THE CHERRY ON TOP

Fulfillment creates epic moments of happiness.

FACT: *You can't be genuinely happy if you are not fulfilled.*

Think about your life as a giant banana split. Imagine a gorgeous crystal dish brimming with banana, strawberry, chocolate, and vanilla ice creams with caramel, hot fudge, whip cream, nuts, and of course, the cherry on top. The banana split represents your life—family, career, and community—and the cherry on top symbolizes happiness. Without the banana split itself, there wouldn't be happiness. You would simply possess a bowl of maraschino cherries. Now I don't know about you, but I can't think of anyone other than a toddler who would want just a bowl of maraschino cherries. The reason we LOVE the cherry on top is because of everything else that comes with it.

True happiness works similarly; happiness is the cherry on top.

Imagine you're on a beach vacation; your spouse accompanies you, and you look over and smile through your umbrella drink and think, "I'm so lucky to be married to this amazing person."

You sit on that beach, umbrella drink in hand, and sense deep joy and gratitude. You feel *happy*. The reason you feel happy is because your marriage is deeply fulfilling. It has required you to be patient, forgiving, tenacious, steadfast, loving, flexible, humble, and committed. *That* is fulfillment. Anyone who tells you they've been "happy" in a marriage 100% of the time is lying. Trust me. I've been married for twenty years and can tell you that although I deeply love my husband, we haven't always been "happy." Like all marriages, we've had a lot of ups and downs. But our steadfast love and commitment to each other and our children make the marriage deeply fulfilling.

> HERE'S A SECRET
>
> *Fulfilling work and relationships create epic moments of happiness. Not the other way around.*

Fulfilling work and relationships create epic moments of happiness. Not the other way around.

Read that again.

As fun as the beach sounds, here's a more common scenario.

You're sitting on the bleachers at your son's little league game. You're there, but you're tired and frazzled. You arrived late because you had to attend a last-minute work meeting that ran past 5:00 pm. That made you late picking up your youngest from daycare, and when you were almost to the ballfield, your husband called and told you to swing by the house to pick up a pair of baseball cleats. Oh, and to top it off, on the way, your youngest child squeezed a packet of ketchup all over the backseat of your freshly cleaned car.

But there you sit on the bleachers, still in your work clothes, waiting for your son's turn at-bat. On his way to the plate, he gazes into the crowd to find you. He makes eye contact, smiles, and gives you that *look*. Every parent knows that look of love and gratitude. It needs no words as the look of "I'm so glad you're here—you're my biggest fan, and I love you" says it all. Suddenly, all of the stuff that was making you frazzled no longer matters. You feel happy. You *are* FULFILLED.

Parenting is one of the best examples of fulfillment—creating epic moments of happiness. Anyone who has raised children knows it's not a perfect or easy process. In fact, it's often the opposite. Right when you think you've got parenting figured out, your kid moves into a new phase. **Nothing marks the passing of time more clearly than raising children.** They grow and change so fast. Sometimes my boys come down for breakfast, and I swear they grew an inch overnight.

Parents will tell you that raising children is the most rewarding and fulfilling job they've ever had, and their children are the joy of their life. But like marriage, raising children requires patience, love, forgiveness, tenacity, and, well, wine. Yes, really good wine.

Cheers to that, friend!

Next time you're feeling frazzled, stressed out, unhappy, or tired, ask yourself, "Is what I'm doing fulfilling?" I promise it will give you the perspective you need to persevere.

YES GIRL, YOU DID THAT!

I find that the harder I work, the

more luck I seem to have.

THOMAS JEFFERSON

YES, GIRL, YOU DID THAT!

Fulfillment Creates Epic Moments of SUCCESS.

There is no such thing as an overnight success story. There is no such thing as an uphill climb without roadblocks, failure, complications, and struggle.

The road to success is often a bumpy one. It's easy to get discouraged on our quest for success because progress rarely happens as fast as we'd like it to. Sometimes we feel disappointed because our plans, lives, relationships, choices, or careers aren't working out like we thought they would. And there are times everything gets so turned around we wonder if we should stay the course.

When the path to success gets tough, focus on how *fulfilling* the progress, effort, journey, or relationship is. We don't walk away from things that are fulfilling to us. We don't quit. We KEEP GOING. We stay the course.

The more fulfilling the journey, the more epic the success. Hard work, perseverance, tenacity, and strength FEEL GOOD. It gives us the power and mental fortitude to press on. THAT IS FULFILLMENT. That promotion you earned at work? It felt good because you worked your ass off for it. That six-figure business you built? It makes you proud because you earned it. That project you've been working on for months is finally complete? Yes, girl, you did that!

When the path is foggy, the bumps in the road cause you to stumble, and road blocks seem to obstruct your way, focus on how fulfilling the journey is and how encouraging it is to make progress.

Someday you'll tell your success story, and it might not sound how you originally envisioned it. But you WILL be able to say:

It wasn't easy, but it was worth it.

Yes, I did that.

Yes, I persevered.

Yes, I believed in myself beyond reason.

Yes, I fell and got back up.

Yes, I kicked ass.

Yes, I earned it.

THE CHRISTMAS EPIPHANY

Death ends a life,

not a relationship.

JACK LEMMON

THE CHRISTMAS EPIPHANY

When I graduated from college, I committed to living a happy and successful life. I was young and eager to create my own life, and I would "choose happiness" every day.

In my early 20s, I married Scott, the love of my life, and pursued a successful career in corporate sales. Everything about my 20s and the life Scott and I had created was incredible. We worked hard during the week and played hard on the weekends. We traveled all the time and became financially independent. Everything about my 20s filled my happiness cup.

In my 30s, I changed careers after we had children. I left my corporate job for a more flexible option and launched a social selling business that enabled me to work from home and create an income doing something I loved. Guess what? This work-life balance made me pretty happy.

A mentor told me that true success is found in happiness. She said, "If you want to create success, you need to create true happiness." So that's what I did. I vigorously pursued happiness. During that time, I read every happiness and self-help book on the market and listened to any pertinent podcast I could find. There was no end to the amount of "happiness" I was seeking to create; I was on a mission, and its name was HAPPY.

As a mom and a wife, I worked to create a happy home. As an executive leader in my social selling business, I measured success with my level of happiness.

When happiness was my muse, I sometimes felt guilty when I felt unhappy. I had to remind myself often: "You are happy and have so much to be happy about."

Like anyone, I had my share of mountains to climb, but for the most part . . . I was living happily every day. Then, something happened that turned my life upside down and drained all my happiness.

I was thirty-eight years old when I received a life-changing phone call informing me my dad died. He was with us one day and suddenly gone the next. He suffered a pulmonary embolism that led to cardiac arrest. I was heartbroken, devastated, and suddenly the unhappiest person I knew.

Dad was my everything: my life, my love, my rock. We loved being together—cooking, shopping, dining, and drinking three olive martinis. We had season tickets to the Kansas City Royals games, and we often went, just to be together.

My boys were six and eight years old at the time, and spending time with "Grandpa Boomer" was always the highlight of their week. To know my dad was to love him. He was a friend to many and had one of the kindest hearts I've ever known. My dad—Mike Johnson—was one of the best.

The news of his death drained all of my happiness. If you've experienced deep levels of grief, you know the darkness and sadness and the struggle to force a smile. You remember the pit in your stomach, burn in your eyes, and ache in your heart. Daily life is challenging, yet you go through the motions every day. If you're like me, you cope by creating a daily ritual and search for the time and space to grieve in private. Even today, the loneliness of the journey weighs heavy. For me, grief has always felt like a solo journey.

During the early stages of my grief, I *tried* to create happiness, but it could not compete with my sadness. In the months after my father's death, I remember wanting ONE thing: I wanted to be happy again. I remember washing the dishes one afternoon and asking myself, "Will I ever really be happy again? Or will this grief continue to consume me?"

Sure, I had moments of happiness, but they were fleeting. And for someone who focused on being happy, not being happy was incredibly frustrating and exhausting.

Many say the first year after losing a loved one is the hardest. You celebrate holidays and traditions for the first time without the person you loved. I was prepared for Christmas to be difficult and sad. I dismissed the thought of it being a joyous holiday with family.

I remember decorating the house, and with every Christmas song, my eyes welled with tears—knowing that dad wouldn't be singing carols with us this year.

Christmas has always been my favorite holiday. I love hosting friends and family in our home. That year, we hosted Christmas for my entire family. And although dad wasn't with us, it turned out to be a pretty magical Christmas.

On Christmas morning, I was surrounded by the people I love most: Scott and my boys, my Mom, my brothers and their families, all the cousins, and my dad's brother and his wife.

Our Christmas mornings are always casual. We make breakfast, open presents, and hang out in our pajamas. We have a tradition of popping champagne on Christmas morning (a tradition I highly recommend).

As we sipped from our fluted glasses and watched the kids tear through presents, we reminisced of Christmases past. To celebrate and remember dad, we hosted a gift exchange in his honor. We bought gifts for each other that dad would have loved, from lottery tickets to grilling utensils to rocks glasses and the finest Scotch. With each unwrapping of a present, we laughed, cried, and recalled the most amazing memories of dad.

At this moment, I had an epiphany: I realized I wasn't necessarily happy, *but I was extremely FULFILLED*. I had a loving family, a flexible career, a community of friends who surrounded

LOVE

never

ENDS

me with love and prayer, and I had a thirty-eight-year relationship with my father that was *everything* to me.

It's been over five years since dad died. And I've discovered another secret about fulfillment:

Fulfilling relationships, work, and memories are unshakeable. Love never ends.

Even the darkest days can't take fulfillment from us. In my darkest days of grief, the relationship with my dad was just as fulfilling as when he was here. And five years later, that love and relationship feel just as fulfilling as it did before he passed away.

> **HERE'S A SECRET**
>
> *Fulfilling relationships, work, and memories are unshakeable. Love never ends.*

I discovered that love is fulfilling and love never ends, and in the process, I stopped chasing happiness and focused on a life of fulfillment. Happiness is fleeting, but fulfillment is steadfast and unshakeable.

If you are on a happiness mission, shift your focus to fulfillment. It's a subtle shift that will change your life. Fulfillment allows you to make tough decisions, enjoy the journey, face your fears, take risks, be courageous, and accept the normal ups and downs of daily life. And nothing can ever take that fulfillment from you.

Trust me, since I've focused on living fulfilled, I've never been happier.

THE SWEATY TOWEL

A dream does not become reality

through magic; it takes sweat,

determination, and hard work.

COLIN POWELL

THE SWEATY TOWEL

Sustainable (adj.): *able to be maintained at a certain rate or level.*

When you shift from pursuing happiness to fulfillment, you'll experience a magical realization: fulfillment is sustainable. In other words, fulfillment can be maintained over the long haul and when times get tough.

We rarely leave fulfilling things behind.
We say "Yes" to fulfilling work and relationships.
We always find time for what is important—our most valuable work, people, and activities.

What is the hardest thing you've ever accomplished? What are the difficult things in life you continue to pursue? I promise you—those moments are where you find fulfillment. That's why fulfillment is sustainable. That's why you show up every day. That's why you keep doing the work.

For me, I pursue the difficult task of consistently exercising and working out. Unless I'm under the weather, I exercise five days a week. And even though I enjoy the feeling of a completed workout, most of the time, I don't WANT to work out. But guess what? I do it anyway.

In the year 2020, it was especially challenging to make myself exercise. As you remember, the COVID-19 pandemic closed gyms for months. And before the pandemic, I was a "group fitness" kinda girl.

I lived at the local Orangetheory Fitness studio. If you haven't taken an Orangetheory Fitness class, I highly recommend trying one. It's a sixty-minute "boot camp" style class that mixes strength and cardiovascular training. It's fast-paced, fun, hard as hell, and incredibly fulfilling. And if you get in a class with a motivating trainer, you're in for an awesome workout.

I'd meet girlfriends for an Orangetheory Fitness workout several times a week. I made friends at the gym and knew all the trainers at my favorite studio. The trainers made the classes FUN, and they pushed you to work hard. They made the challenging workout something I looked forward to doing multiple times a week. I lived for their encouragement, push, playlists, and fun. It was hard work, but I always left feeling invigorated, accomplished, and fulfilled.

Trying to recreate that energy while exercising at home was challenging. There was no late fee if I didn't show up to class. There were no friends to meet for the workout. There wasn't a coach pushing me to run faster and lift heavy.

I had to shift my mindset and focus on what mattered most about the workouts. What mattered most was showing up and how I felt AFTER the workout was completed. The fulfillment wasn't in meeting friends (let's face it, meeting for happy hour is just as fun and not as much work); it was in starting and finishing the workout itself. It was rewarding to put in the work, even when I didn't want to.

This kind of exercise is fulfilling. If you don't exercise at least three times a week, I dare you to start today. No, I *double-dog* dare you. Commit to working out three times a week for three months. I promise you'll love the way you feel. Even if you hate doing the work, you'll experience fulfillment. And if you fall off the wagon and stop exercising after three months, remind yourself of what you accomplished. I have a hunch you'll miss the feeling so much that you might even start exercising again.

Next time you're doing something HARD or CHALLENG-ING, something that is PUSHING or CHANGING you, some-thing that makes you want to throw in the sweaty towel, walk away, and quit, ask yourself if it is fulfilling. If it is, keep doing it. Fulfilling things are sustainable, and you can do hard things.

And if you're doing something that is not fulfilling, give your-self permission to throw in the sweaty towel and move onto some-thing that provides sustainable, long-lasting fulfillment. You de-serve nothing less.

VIEW FROM THE TOP

Today is your day!

Your mountain is waiting, so . . .

get on your way!

DR. SEUSS

VIEW FROM THE TOP

One of the most curious things about fulfilling work is that it *CREATES ENERGY*. Fulfilling work keeps us coming back for more. A simple definition of the word *energizing* is "*to give life, vigor, or spirit to*."

Think about something that you've done that was challenging but incredibly fulfilling. In the last chapter, I shared my fitness journey with you. The workouts are never easy but incredibly energizing. No matter how exhausted, sweaty, or sore I might be, I still go back for more workouts.

Have you ever climbed a mountain? I haven't (and I have *zero* desire to do so), but I have several friends who have not only climbed one mountain, but MANY MOUNTAINS—I'm talking literally here, not figuratively.

If you ever want to hear a great story, ask someone who's climbed a mountain to tell you about their adventure. Their story will be filled with trials, tribulations, injury, and fear. They will tell you about the taxing weather conditions and severe health complications that forced some to stay at base camp while others continued the climb. They will tell you about blisters, sunburns, cold, stress, hunger, and exhaustion.

And then they will tell you in vivid detail about the view from the top. They will share with you how magnificent the experience was and how rewarding it was to reach the peak. They will get out their smartphone to show you the pictures they took on the highest peak of the tallest mountain and tell you how fulfilling it was to make it to the top.

And then they will probably tell you what their NEXT mountain adventure will be. Why on earth would they want to engage in such a risky and treacherous climb *again*? It's simple: the climb is incredibly fulfilling and energizing and keeps them coming back for more.

NOT ALL TIME IS CREATED EQUAL

---

*We think, mistakenly, that success
is the result of the amount of time
we put in at work, instead of the
quality of time we put in.*

ARIANA HUFFINGTON

NOT ALL TIME IS CREATED EQUAL

Time. The one thing we wish we had more of and the one resource we can't get back once we invest, spend, or waste it.

Unfortunately, time is not something we get to manipulate. We all get the same 24 hours each day and 365 days a year. But how we choose to spend those hours is up to us.

HERE'S A SECRET: not all time is created equal.

Read that again. *Out loud.*

One of the most significant struggles working women encounter is work-life balance. I've surveyed thousands of women, and on a scale of 1-5 (1 being completely "out of balance" and 5 being "no issues with balance"), the average is 3. on the scale. Therefore, even if you're a 5, you likely know multiple women who need some support.

> Balance (noun) : *A condition in which different elements are equal or in the correct proportions.*

> Balance (verb) : *To offset or compare the value of (one thing) with another.*

When struggling with work-life balance, we often evaluate it and measure it with time. I'll be honest; work-life balance wasn't an issue for me until I had kids. For most working moms, we aren't prepared for the feelings that come with learning to navigate career and motherhood. When I was pregnant with my first child, I remember thinking, "I'll hire a nanny, continue to travel for work, and have amazing weekends as a family. It'll be the best of all worlds." And yes, I was that matter of fact about it. Little did I know having a child would change everything. I had no idea how much I would struggle with work-life balance.

When we had our first son, my fulfilling career butted heads with my new and fulfilling role as a mom. They felt in competition with each other. When I was traveling for my job, I felt guilty about not being with my boys. And then, when I was with the boys, I felt guilty for not working. And at all times, I felt like I might be "missing out" on something.

I had to learn that fulfilling things should not compete and do not need to compete. There is no need to compare fulfilling endeavors. You can't measure fulfillment with time. *Fulfillment is what happens within and over time. It's how you show up. It's what you make of it. It's about being present, being intentional and releasing expectations.*

Let me give you an example. My husband has an incredible relationship with our sons. He also has an extremely demanding twelve-hour workday. Most days, he's gone before they're out of bed and arrives home around dinner. But he always takes time to connect with them at the end of his long workday. Maybe they'll shoot hoops, throw a baseball around, or play a game. It's typically around an hour a day, but that hour is 100% focused time. He's fully present and engaged. It's FULFILLING for him, and it's fulfill-

> **HERE'S A SECRET**
>
> *Fulfilling things should not compete and do not need to compete.*

ing for the boys. His full attention for that one hour is worth way more than a half-hearted presence for an entire afternoon.

In many cases and most relationships, focusing on fulfillment eliminates the need for balance in your schedule. Not all time is created equal.

Next time you're struggling with balance, ask yourself if what you're doing is fulfilling. If it's not fulfilling, stop saying yes to stuff you don't want to do. More often than not, we experience imbalance because we have over-extend ourselves. We aren't assertive when we need to be. Set rigid boundaries and stick to them. It's okay to say "no" to stuff that isn't fulfilling.

> *Is being a room mom at the school fulfilling to you?*
> *Is being on that committee at work fulfilling to you?*
> *Is meeting your girlfriends for dinner fulfilling to you?*

Is taking sixty minutes to exercise fulfilling to you?

If so, keep doing it. If not, stop doing it.

Balance is about how you spend your time and how you show up. You *can* have it all—you *can* have the career, a social life you love, and an amazing relationship with your spouse and children. Fulfilling things are not in competition. You can love your career and love your children. Your passions are your purpose, and your purpose is love. Love does not compete.

CHANGE YOUR HAIR, CHANGE YOUR MIND

Life is a series of natural and spontaneous changes. Don't resist them; that only creates sorrow. Let reality be reality. Let things flow naturally forward in whatever way they like.

LAO TZU

CHANGE YOUR HAIR, CHANGE YOUR MIND

HERE'S A SECRET: It's okay to change. Because one thing is certain: you will NEVER arrive. We are always a work in progress.

There will be ups and downs, but you're never going to "arrive" at some pinnacle in life and then coast to the end. Who you were is not who you came to be. Who you are today is not who you came to be. And this is not a bad thing, as there's always an opportunity to level up. You are always going to be a work in progress. How beautiful it is to know the best is ALWAYS yet to come.

> HERE'S A SECRET
>
> *It's okay to change. Because one thing is certain: you will NEVER arrive. We are always a work in progress.*

Change your hair.
Change your mind.
Change your career.

Change your style.
Change your life.

Change can be incredibly scary. Let's face it; even a hairstyle change can seem like a huge life decision. Trust me, I *know*. I've cut my hair many times, and I've contemplated cutting bangs for over twenty years. Come to think of it, I've never had a friend cut their hair without giving it serious thought and consulting close friends. If changing your hair is scary, you understand how scary BIG life changes can be.

I've changed my career three times, our home four times, and my style changes constantly. Just like style, you will never "arrive." Right when you think you've got it figured out, it's time for a change. Remember when you swore you couldn't pull off skinny jeans? And now you've been rocking them for ten years only to find out they are no longer "in." Style and fashion change, and so do you. Change is inevitable.

> *"Be who you came to be" is your permission slip to grow, change, and evolve.*

"Be who you came to be" is your permission slip to grow, change, and evolve.

Earlier in the book, I advised you to focus on fulfilling work and relationships and then show up fully present and engaged in those spaces. Understand that those spaces can and will change. Work that was once deeply fulfilling might not be fulfilling anymore. Most of us have been in relationships (love or friendship) that at some point were no longer fulfilling.

This type of change is hard. Big life changes, like career and relationships, can be extremely challenging. I just want you to remember that it's okay to change. Who you were is not who you came to be. Sometimes this type of change can be so complicated and confusing we might start to feel like it's "bad" or even "wrong." Not true! It's not bad or wrong if a job or relationship that was once really fulfilling is no longer fulfilling. It just means something changed, and you are moving into a new chapter of your life.

Like most, I've been through career and relationship changes. In my 20's I was climbing the corporate ladder and was confident that I was going all the way to the top. Both the leadership team and my managers told me I was tracking for C-suite success, the idea of which kept me incredibly determined and fulfilled. My work was my life.

At the same time, my maternal clock was ticking. Scott and I had been married for six years, and we knew we wanted to start a family in our 30s. I wanted to be a mom and was certain that I would be fulfilled by hiring a nanny, continuing my rigorous travel schedule, and expanding my executive leadership role at the company.

WE ARE

ALWAYS

A WORK

PROGRESS

There's a saying: "You don't know what you don't know."

I was forever changed after my first son was born. All of the familiar sources of success and fulfillment weren't as rewarding. The job I loved was no longer where I wanted to spend most of my time. I still wanted to work and invest in my career, but I wanted flexibility in my schedule to be more present with my children. Never in a million years did I think I would bust my ass climbing the corporate ladder to leave it all behind and start a home-based business. But I did.

It was one of the most challenging decisions I ever made. Not only was I fearful of leaving everything I worked so hard to achieve, but I was also worried about what other people would think of me. One of the most challenging aspects of change is the fear of what others are going to think. The fear of judgment can be one of the most complicated aspects to navigate during a season of change.

A big change will uncover your faithful supporters and friends. If someone is talking negatively about you or a personal choice you have made, they do not deserve a spot in your inner circle. Treat your life like a concert. Keep your raving fans in the front row. Don't give good seats to people who belong in the nosebleed section. You can control who you're listening to and taking advice from. You also don't need approval from friends and extended family on all of your life decisions. I am guessing that you don't love every decision that others make, so there is no need for everyone to love your choices. It was my husband who reminded me, "Who cares what anyone else thinks of your decisions. We know why you're making this big change. And that's enough." What matters most and who matters most will always matter most.

Just as fulfilling work can change, fulfilling relationships can change. Change in friendships and relationships can be extremely challenging to navigate. Most of us have been there—the life-changing breakup, the "one" who turned out not to be the "one," the friendship that came to an end. I'm sure you can still recall the first time you had a broken heart. And I'm also sure you got through it or are getting through it.

When we love and trust others, we become vulnerable to heartbreak and grief. A sad truth in life is that not all friendships and relationships will last a lifetime. That is because not all people grow and change together.

Have you ever had a friend you were close with but over time, it just kind of fizzled out? Most likely, one of you changed. Change often impacts relationships and friendships. I have been there, and I know it's hard to navigate.

Was it me?

Was it her?

What really happened?

Why aren't we ride-or-die besties?

What I found is that there is no need for a story or narrative on who, what, or why the friendship changed. It's enough that it just changed. Maybe it was you that changed. Perhaps it was her that changed. It is possible both of you changed.

You can still celebrate that friendship for everything that it was and celebrate the women both of you have become. Just because you aren't "ride-or-die besties" anymore doesn't mean the friendship wasn't special and important. Celebrate you. Celebrate her. And celebrate the woman you've become.

Life is entirely too short not to pursue fulfilling work and relationships. When change occurs in these spaces, it doesn't invalidate them. Celebrate the work and friendships that were once incredibly fulfilling. They made you the woman you are today.

WRITE
YOUR
STORY

Remember that you're a living,

breathing novel, literally writing

your own story. Your very own

authentically personal piece of art.

It's pretty glorious.

VICTORIA ERICKSON

WRITE YOUR STORY

The mantra "Be who you came to be" means you're always a work in progress—a state of beautiful transformation and change. The mantra is your permission slip to grow, change and evolve personally and professionally.

Who you were in the past isn't who you came to be.
Who you are today isn't who you came to be.

Your life will continue to unfold and evolve daily. **You write your story one day at a time.**

Stay focused on what is fulfilling to YOU. The things that are fulfilling to you convey LOVE.

Love will guide you.

Be who you CAME to be.

PART

Two

OWN IT

Most people are other people.

Their thoughts are someone else's

opinions, their lives a mimicry,

their passions a quotation. Be

yourself; everyone else is taken.

OSCAR WILDE

INSTAGLAM

&

FAKEBOOK

The reason we struggle with

insecurity is because we compare

our behind-the-scenes with

everyone else's highlight reel.

PASTOR STEVE FURTICK

INSTAGLAM & FAKEBOOK

We live in a social media-driven world.

According to the creative agency, We Are Social, on average, internet users spend two hours and twenty-two minutes a day on social media.[1] We turn to social media for updates on our friends and family, shopping, leisure, laughter, and daily news. Let's face it, we're curious about what others are up to and what they think about what's going on in the world.

Sometimes we scroll for entertainment, sometimes we scroll for curiosity, sometimes we scroll for validation, and sometimes we scroll only to end up comparing our lives to others. We should all know this by now: don't compare yourself to others. But it's hard not to compare ourselves to others on social media, especially when we see the highlight reels of others' lives (more on that in a moment).

"Fakebook" and "Instaglam," as I like to call them, are where we see only the best of our friends and followers. We see the wins, highs, vacations, accolades, achievements, and the perfect picture, but rarely the mess. In total transparency, I participate as much as anyone. I take multiple shots trying to capture the perfect "gram-worthy" photo and enjoy sharing my personal, professional, and parenting achievements on Facebook. Most days, I really enjoy social media; I'm always curious to see what everyone is up to, and I enjoy celebrating their achievements. More often than not, social media can be light and fun. For the most part, it feels good, and we like to share our wins, shine light on our family, and celebrate progress.

But for the many successes we celebrate in our lifetime, remember this SECRET: behind any polished post on Instagram, you have no idea what battle anyone is fighting.

HERE'S A SECRET

Behind any polished post on Instagram, you have no idea what battle anyone is fighting.

Even in our beautiful filtered photos, our "behind the scenes" is often a beautiful mess.

The Secrets I'm sharing in Part Two explore the balance of embracing your authentic self while respecting the authenticity of others.

Here's a little hint and reminder: any time you start doubting yourself and who you came to be, revisit these secrets. You are authentic and perfectly flawed. There is only one you. Own It.

HIGHS & LOWS OF HIGHLIGHT REELS

Too many people overvalue what

they are not and undervalue what

they are.

MALCOLM S. FORBES

HIGHS & LOWS OF HIGHLIGHT REELS

In the year 2020—between the global pandemic, the election, racial tensions, and widespread protesting—we learned social media could get pretty ugly pretty quick. We discovered that words and opinions become divisive and often leave us feeling appalled and angry.

In an attempt to remain optimistic and keep our social media fun and carefree, the majority of us stick with the highlight reels. We share the best, the funny, and the highs. And let's face it, we love a highlight reel. We love to laugh, relate, and celebrate.

As much as we love showcasing the perfect moments, they can spark thoughts of comparison. Sometimes we consciously compare, but often we subconsciously compare. And we're left to wonder, "Am I enough?"

We compare ourselves to others.

We compare our lives.

We compare our relationships.

We compare our success.

We compare our bodies.

We compare our homes, cars, fashion, marriages, children, and careers. And the list goes on.

Although comparing isn't what you set out to do, you're only human, and questioning and comparing yourself to others is common. But when you compare your reality to another person's highlight reel, you're not doing yourself any favors. These unfair comparisons bring up feelings of inadequacy and insecurity.

HERE'S A SECRET

YES, YOU are ENOUGH.

I want you to know this "Secret" and I want you to plant it inside your soul. YES, YOU are ENOUGH. You are perfectly flawed, beautiful, celebrated, seen, and capable.

Day-to-day reality and someone's highlight reel are vastly different lenses. Don't lose perspective of who you came to be based on someone else's social media reel.

Most of all, you have to remember, You didn't come to be her; you came to be you. It doesn't matter what anyone else is up to because you came to be YOU—not them.

So shine your beautiful, perfectly flawed, and authentic light.

THE SOCIAL DILEMMA

There's nothing more daring than showing up, putting ourselves out there and letting ourselves be seen.

BRENÉ BROWN

THE SOCIAL DILEMMA

Our authenticity is being stolen from us daily as we live in fear of others' scorn.

In a time where we preach fairness, equality, equity, and authenticity—we've never been more afraid to show up without armor. It seems everyone wants to advise you on who to be, how to talk, how to think, what to post online, and how to show up in person.

On social media, all content is under a magnifying glass and up for criticism. Random strangers don't hesitate to tell you what you should or should not post, share, or write. Don't let others shatter your authenticity. Don't let them marginalize who you came to be.

> *Be who you came to be. Love will guide you.*

"Be who you came to be. Love will guide you."

That is the message. That is your mission. LOVE will guide you. At the core of all of us is LOVE. If you are leading your life from a place of love, and someone makes you feel ashamed or misunderstood, that's on them and not you. I'm giving you permission to be who YOU came to be.

What if you showed up exactly as you desire? What if you didn't fear failure, judgment, unacceptance, backlash, or hate? Stop watering down your authenticity to please others.

No one has a responsibility to use their social platform for something that isn't authentic to them. You aren't required to speak out on current affairs or share your political views unless that feels good and authentic to YOU. Be who you came to be. And if weighing in on current affairs doesn't feel good or isn't the authentic you, then don't do it.

Making the world a better place isn't done by judging those who don't share worldly or political views. It's done by giving others space and respect to be who they came to be and let LOVE guide them.

Similarly, let LOVE guide you. What do you love? What are you passionate about? And how does that LOVE transcend to make the world a better place? Express that!

You love makeup.

You love to share makeup stories and tips; that's not shallow. You're helping women feel better about themselves, highlight their beauty, and show up with confidence.

LOVE

WILL

guide

YOU

You love cooking.

You love to share your food with friends. Food brings us together. Food ignites the senses and nourishes the soul. Your food posts and passions give your followers recipe ideas to cook and nourish the ones they love.

You love to exercise.

You love sharing your workouts and results. That's not self-indulgent. Your body is a temple. You're encouraging others to embrace their strength to focus on health and meaningful activities.

You love your kids.

You love bragging about them and posting pictures of them. AMEN Mamma! Always shine light on your children.

You love decorating your home.

You love posting pics of your interior design projects and home décor. You're not bragging. It's your space where you create love and life for your family.

You love fashion.

You love sharing images of you in different outfits and finds. How wonderful you are confident enough with your body to share your fashion and style.

You love your job.

You post about your company and share accolades you've earned. Good for you. You're making a positive impact and earning an income doing something you love. That's the American dream.

You love your dog.

You post pictures of him daily. Dog lovers unite. We're here for it!

You love volunteering.

You love helping others in need. Shine that beautiful light.

You love politics.

You love sharing your political views. Good for you. If it's politics you're passionate about, share that!

Here's the bottom line: your passions are not small, and you shouldn't ignore them. Share what you LOVE. Your social media platform is YOUR platform, and you should share what you're passionate about! No one is forced to follow you, and you are not forced to follow anyone.

So please stop overthinking your next selfie. Snap it and share it! Share what you LOVE. Allow others to share what THEY love. You came to be YOU. They came to be THEM.

LOVE will guide you: that is a secret worth sharing.

PUT ON THE THE SKATES

———————————

Our greatest glory

is not in never falling but in rising

every time we fall.

———————————

CONFUCIUS

PUT ON THE SKATES

Fall. Get up. Fall. Get up. Fall. Get up.

In the winter of 2018, we took our boys ice skating for the first time. Here's how the night went: they fell, and then they got right back up. And they did this over and over.

It wasn't a super-cold night, but with each fall, their pants and gloves got wetter from the melting ice. The cold air, wet clothes, and lack of skill didn't faze them. With every fall, they rose again. They laughed and smiled with each wipeout and pulled themselves up with a fierce determination to make it around the rink.

By the end of the night, their cheeks were freezing, butts were sore, and their pants were soaking wet. But their resolve to ice-skate was on fire. After skating for a few hours, we decided to treat the boys to hot chocolate (and hot toddies for us). While we sipped our piping hot drinks, the boys gushed about how much fun they had at the rink. My husband and I praised them for sticking with it. We were proud of them for getting back up time and time again and never complaining about the cold. We loved their tenacity, attitude, and determination to learn this new skill.

Not once did they express discouragement. Not once did they talk about quitting.

They both exchanged their skates for a different pair at one point that evening—convinced their constant falling was an equipment error. I can't blame them. Magic skates would have been the ultimate fix. But nothing slowed them down. Even their sore butts and iced-over pants. They loved everything about the experience. And the next day? They woke up early, and the first thing they asked was, "Can we go ice skating today?"

I reflected a lot on that experience in the weeks that followed. New challenges create new opportunities for failure and success. Starting something new is never easy. It tests our resolve, determination, tenacity, and character. It takes courage to fight the fear. It takes a steadfast belief that it's worth it. It takes a steadfast belief that we are worth it.

HERE'S A SECRET

There is a learning curve for everything.

There is a learning curve for everything.

As adults, it's hard to ride the learning curve. Often, we want to be on the other side of the curve from day one. When we put big dreams and goals into action, we become vulnerable to failure. Because dreaming and planning involve risk, our fears are ignited. We question if we ever should have "put on skates" in the first place with each failure or fall. We doubt our ability, talent, and the ensuing path forward.

ENJOY THE EXPERIENCE & EACH

fall

Personal achievements create significant fulfillment. And these achievements take time—and A LOT of failures. To discover your purpose—which REQUIRES many failures—is a success!

What if you faced your fears, took risks, and embraced failure more like my boys did when they learned to skate?

They relished the experience and all of the ups and downs. They never expected to become champions the first night out; they just wanted to learn how to skate. They didn't care what other people thought every time they wiped out; they focused on getting back on their feet. They never questioned if they could even learn how to skate; their vision of skating was more significant than any fall.

We went skating again just a few days later, and they continued to fall, over and over and over. And they continued to try, again and again. Their determination was fierce.

Enjoy the experience and each fall. Get up, and know that you'll fall again and again. (And again.) Appreciate the journey. One day you'll reminisce about how far you've come.

And I promise you won't even remember the cold.

YOU DIDN'T COME TO BE HER

Trying to be someone else is a

waste of the person you are.

MARILYN MONROE

YOU DIDN'T COME TO BE HER

Whether you compare yourself to someone and it makes you feel great, or you compare yourself to someone and it makes you feel bad . . . it's a complete waste of your time and energy because you are benchmarking yourself against someone else.

HERE'S A SECRET: you didn't come to be more like her; you came to be YOU.

We love to compare things. We compare restaurants, movies, vacations, and food. We compare cities, sports, and schools. As parents, we even find ourselves

> HERE'S A SECRET
>
> *You didn't come to be more like her; you came to be YOU.*

unfairly comparing our children to their siblings or other kids. I'm not sure why we compare our children, as we love them unconditionally. We love their quirks, talents, minds, and most of all, their love and individuality. As a mother, I remind myself to honor their authenticity and let them be who THEY came to be. They didn't come to be who I want them to be; they came to be who God intended them to be. And just like our children didn't come to be more like someone else's kid—you didn't come to be more like another woman.

You didn't come to be her. You came to be YOU. There is no reason you should compare yourself to another woman. I know it's easier said than done, as we want to make sure we're "enough."

Am I a good enough Mom?

Am I good enough at my job?

Am I a good enough wife?

Am I enough?

Often, when we seek a sense of validation through comparing, we just feel small and insufficient in the end.

You are enough.

Read that again.

Now repeat after me: "I am enough."

You are where you're supposed to be. Honor your authenticity. Honor your talents and gifts. Give yourself the grace to grow, change, and evolve. Celebrate your story—the ups and downs—and that you've always had the strength to persevere.

Keep shining your beautiful, authentic light. Be the woman YOU came to be.

ADMIRE HER

I've always believed that one

woman's success can only help

another woman's success.

GLORIA VANDERBILT

ADMIRE HER

Here's the secret to once-and-for-all eliminating comparison from your life: comparison doesn't have to be a bad thing—it's all about how you're looking at "her" as another woman pursuing her dreams. Less comparing, more admiring.

We often compare because there is something we want or desire. We want to take our lives to the next level, so we start looking around to see what everyone else is doing and what is possible.

Next time you find yourself in comparison, *shift to admiration.*

Comparison *ignites feelings of inadequacy, insecurity, and self-doubt.*

Admiration *ignites the sense of celebration and possibility.*

Admire HER. Celebrate another woman's achievements and authenticity. Celebrate what she's accomplished and shine your light on HER.

If she can do it—you can do it.

Admiration ignites confidence. There is nothing more powerful than a confident woman. Confident women empower other women. Confident women ignite belief and self-confidence in other women.

HERE'S A SECRET

If she can do it—you can do it.

ADMIRE HER. Celebrate her strengths, achievements, authenticity, and individuality.

ADMIRE YOU. Celebrate your strengths, achievements, authenticity, and individuality.

You didn't come to be HER. You came to be YOU.

YOUR STORY IS **YOUR** STORY.

Stop thinking you're doing it all wrong. Your path doesn't look like anybody else's because it can't, it shouldn't, and it won't.

ELEANOR BROWNN

YOUR STORY IS YOUR STORY.

Consider this: Your start might be someone else's end. Your midway might take an unexpected turn. What takes you two years might take someone else five.

Don't ever compare your story to another woman's story—it's not supposed to look, feel, or be the same.

One of the problems of comparing our story to others is we genuinely have no idea where someone is in their story. We have no clue what they've been through and what their

> **HERE'S A SECRET**
>
> *Don't ever compare your story to another woman's story—it's not supposed to look, feel, or be the same.*

end-game is. And even if you DID know all the plot twists, turns, and wild details . . . it doesn't matter. That's HER story. Your story is your story.

A CAREER STORY

I love summer sales conferences. They are full of excitement, innovation, and recognition. Sales professionals from all over the world gather to learn about the new products, initiatives, and strategies the company will pursue in the coming year and celebrate all of the achievements from the prior one. And if you know salespeople, they are often a vibrant group of "fun makers" who aren't afraid to cut loose and have a good time.

In my career, these conferences were attended by the most seasoned and respected sales professionals as well as the "green" sales reps seeking to immerse themselves in the company culture.

Years ago, I attended a sales conference in Las Vegas (my favorite conference city), and I roomed with a friend who had always been an "A Player." I joked that she could sell ice to an Eskimo. She never just "hit" her sales goals, she knocked them out of the park. During the prior year, not only did she CRUSH her sales targets, but she had her first child and was doing the "working mom" thing brilliantly.

After a day full of a flurry of activity, including an awards banquet and party, we finally had a moment to put our feet up and reflect on the day. She seemed a little quiet; I thought she just missed her baby. So, like any good friend, I asked her what was up. To my surprise, she shared with me that she felt a little small at the conference this year and that this year was the first year she was not recognized as "Top 10 in Sales" in the company.

Surprised, I said, "GIRL, STOP! Not only did you hit your targets, but you also made a human! And you did both with style and grace!"

I had to remind her about her year. In addition to crushing it at her job, she had a baby *and* moved into a new house. What an extraordinary year she had! There was so much to celebrate. Her success wasn't measured on "Top 10 Sales Professionals in the Company;" it was measured on her personal and professional accomplishments.

She was benchmarking her success on others' expectations and was robbing herself of being present and enjoying her own success and journey.

As a mother, I've found that comparison starts at a young age. Young children are curious about how they fit in and rank amongst their peers. This type of competition can serve its purpose by guiding our children to pursue what they love, where they have natural talent, and what they are willing to dedicate time to. But ultimately, their only competition in life is themselves. They didn't come to be better than someone else; they came to be the very best version of themselves.

A PARENTING STORY

My boys have tried almost every sport; soccer, basketball, tennis, track and field, football, gymnastics, swim team and baseball. It was a great way for them to discover what they liked, and more importantly, what sport was fulfilling to them.

I remember when Jack was on the summer swim team. (If your kids have ever been on a swim team, you know this is a serious summer commitment.) The daily practices last for several hours, and there is at least one meet a week that can last up to eight hours. Jack was "all-in" that summer. And he was a pretty great little swimmer.

During one of his first races, I noticed he kept popping his head out of the water to look around and see where the other swimmers were. And every time he did this, it slowed him down. Each time he raised his head up, he added seconds to his race time. Like any eight-year-old swimmer, he was really bummed that he didn't place at that meet.

Afterward, we talked about it. I told him that he needed to focus on his strokes and that looking around wasn't going to help him finish the race. In fact, this was slowing his performance. Of course, like most children, he didn't really like hearing sports advice from his mother. He didn't believe that he was popping his head out to "look around," but after reviewing his videos, he realized what he was doing.

So the next week at practice, he focused on what he could control— his strokes, breathing, and transitions. And then he put all of that practice to work at the next meet. And not only did he take eight seconds off his race time, but he also took home first place.

YOUR STORY

Your story is your story. There is no need to look around to see how it compares to someone else's. They aren't living your life, and you aren't living theirs. Your end might be their start. Their start might be your middle.

Just be you.

Be present.

Show up.

Chin up.

Put in the work.

Shine your light.

Celebrate your wins.

Throw in a plot twist.

Just write your story.

You didn't come this far to compare your journey to someone else's. Keep writing YOUR story . . . one day at a time.

IT'S OK
TO NOT
BE OK

Grieving doesn't make you
imperfect. It makes you human.

SARAH DESSEN

IT'S OKAY
TO NOT BE OKAY

I know you've been there. We've all been there.

You're down.

You're tired.

You're defeated.

You're deflated.

You've lost something.

You've lost someone.

And instead of giving yourself permission to FEEL whatever it is you're feeling, you put a bandage on the emotional wound and tell yourself, "It could be worse." You benchmark your mental state on someone who has it "worse" than you. Brené Brown calls this "comparative suffering," and it's one of the most damaging mindsets.

I've been there.

After my Dad died, someone said to me, "At least it wasn't one of your children." (Insert shock, dismay, heartbreak, and anger.) Not only did those words fuel my grief—they made it worse. I started thinking about all the parents who have lost a child, and I started feeling bad for how distraught I was over my father's death.

Just like benchmarking someone else's wins to your current state only hurts, benchmarking your losses also hurts. We can never truly understand how someone else is feeling. We can be empathetic, thoughtful, kind, and caring. But we can't actually feel what they're feeling.

This is your permission slip to feel whatever it is you're feeling.

If you're sad—*it's okay to be sad.*

If you're tired—*It's okay to be tired.*

If you're just down—*it's okay to be down.*

But whatever you do, don't shame yourself or benchmark your suffering on someone else's suffering. Feel whatever it is you're feeling—then choose how to deal with it.

Ask yourself this question: Do I want to put a bandage on my feelings because someone else has it worse, or do I want to go through the healing process of sadness and grief?

Five years after my dad died, I told myself, "This is the year. This is the year I'm not going to be sad on September 14th. This year, I'm not falling back into grief on the anniversary of his death. This year, I'm going to celebrate and remember him with joy instead of sadness." And that year—the fifth anniversary of his death—I was on my knees, succumbing to a wave of grief that hit the *hardest* since I answered the phone and learned of his death. It was as if the universe was saying, "Grief and love never end!"

Tears, exhaustion, grief, and sadness are the way we heal. We must give ourselves space to FEEL. My life coach, Heather White, told me that trying to avoid feelings of sadness and grief is like trying to hold in food poisoning. You just can't do it. Mourning and grief are the body's way of cleansing itself. Sadness, grief, crying and exhaustion are part of the process of healing and renewal. It's all part of the cycle of LOVE. Love never ends. Grief never ends.

HERE'S A SECRET

Tears, exhaustion, grief, and sadness are the way we heal.

What you *can* control is how you treat your mind and body during grief, sadness, and uncertain times. Are you shaming yourself? Bandaging your emotions with comparative suffering? Masking your grief because "it's been too long" or "it could be worse."

If so, from here on out, STOP.

Grief is a ritual. Give yourself space and permission to feel it. You must give yourself the time and space to grieve. Sit in the feelings for however long you need, and then do something GOOD for your heart, soul, and mind.

Go to lunch with a friend.

Take a long walk.

Get plenty of rest.

Even during the hardest times, feel ALL the feelings.

May we all repeat on a regular basis, "I'm only human."

Be who you came to be. Life is not a cakewalk. Our deepest sadness and grief are reserved for that which we care most deeply about. When you are overwhelmed by the pain, be authentic to yourself, allow yourself to feel all of it, and in doing so, you honor the people and circumstances most dear to you. It was something or someone that was incredibly FULFILLING to you.

It was LOVE.

SECRET NINETEEN

THREE

INCH

HEELS

I'm not afraid of heights, have you

seen my shoes?

CARRIE BRADSHAW

THREE INCH HEELS

Anaïs Nin says, "We do not see things as they are, we see them as we are."

Read that again.

YES, your PERCEPTION is your reality.

But seriously, who are we to judge? What is our baseline? What makes us the expert on how someone else should show up? Why do we get to weigh in on who they came to be? I've done it. You've done it. We've all done it. Guilty as charged.

Most of the time, we don't even realize we're judging. Our subconscious mind is always filtering information. Have you ever experienced a deep boredom that leads to observing others around you? Judgment subtly plays itself out in one of mankind's favorite past times: people-watching.

One of my favorite places to people-watch is at a busy airport. I wonder who the people are, where they're from and where they are going. Are they traveling for business or pleasure? What are they looking at on their laptop? Who are they talking to on the phone? Are they in love or lonely? And why in the hell did they choose those three-inch heels to wear in the airport? (The footwear choices I see at airports and theme parks often blow my mind. Lol.)

I try not to judge, but like all of us, I do.

People-watching is entertaining and is ultimately a self-indulgent form of judgment. We make assumptions, write their stories, and try to figure out strangers. Sadly, these judgments come from outer appearance; everything from looks, age, race, hair color, body type, fashion, and yes . . . even footwear.

HERE'S A SECRET

Judgment of others is simply a reflection of yourself.

Judgment of others is simply a reflection of yourself.

I'm not encouraging you to shame yourself for people watching. Go ahead and keep doing it. But next time you judge someone, use it as a chance to reflect on yourself. What does each passing thought say about you? Then flip the judgment to admiration. Admire them for who they came to be. Admire them for their authenticity. Admire them for showing up. Admire them for being bold enough to wear heels to a theme park.

Proceed with KINDNESS. We never truly know what's going on behind the scenes.

Less judgment. More admiration.

ROSE-COLORED GLASSES

You live life looking forward,

you understand life looking

backward.

SOREN KIERKEGAARD

ROSE-COLORED GLASSES

October 2014

It was 8:30 a.m. on a typical Wednesday. I'd been up for three hours, all of the usual weekday "stuff".

My typical morning routine consists of fifty squats and a ten-minute meditation. I make the bed, unload the dishwasher, wake up my boys (if they aren't already up), pick out their clothes, brush their hair, feed them, and make lunches. Then we review all the homework assignments before I take the boys to school. And sometimes, I have time to sneak in some social media posts.

On this particular morning, I arrived early to a breakfast meeting with a former colleague-turned-friend. This is my definition of early morning productivity and success.

She is a kindred spirit, and I always enjoy our time together. I love hearing about her success, her business, and updates on her children and family. No matter how many great things she and I have going on in our current lives, we *always* reminisce about our time working together when we were in our 20s.

Our lives could not be any more different now than they were

REMAIN

present

back then. Back in our corporate days, we were both newlyweds, didn't have kids, and hadn't lived through any major life events. We hadn't even purchased homes. In fact, our biggest expenses at the time were probably the overpriced handbags we were carrying.

In our 20s we worked for a fast-paced sales organization that required long hours and a lot of travel. The thrill of presenting at executive meetings and landing big accounts made us welcome the early mornings and late nights at the office. The travel schedule was rigorous, but we never turned down a weekday happy hour. We traveled the country, made a lot of money, and celebrated a lot of wins.

After breakfast, as I drove home, I thought about how I've always romanticized the work I did in my late 20s. I have to remind myself: don't get swept away in nostalgia.

With every year of life, we evolve, and so does our purpose, focus, and priorities. We get older, and our lives get more intricate. Our marriages become more complex with the addition of children. Our careers change, our families get bigger, and our community of friends and colleagues expands.

What used to work in our lives doesn't always work anymore, and the change is often challenging. But I find that it is often nostalgia that makes the change difficult.

We put the idea of success on a pedestal and remember the good times. It's human nature to be nostalgic, but nostalgia can be a form of self-deception that idealizes our experiences. It's easy to look at the past through rose-colored glasses. But is that reality or some kind of distortion? It's often hard to distinguish between the two because we get wrapped up in the nostalgia of how things "used to be."

Rather than returning to the past, we need to remain present while enjoying the memories and celebrating how far we've come. Our past is part of the journey to "being who you came to be". Don't let your rose-colored glasses distract you from being mindful and present. If you focus on the past for too long, you'll miss another wonderful morning filled with family prep, taking kids to school, and even making your bed.

NEVER MAKE DECISIONS BASED ON NOSTALGIA

Nostalgia is a seductive liar.

GEORGE BALL

NEVER MAKE DECISIONS BASED ON NOSTALGIA

Let's take the battle against nostalgia one step further and consider the science behind this phenomenon. There are numerous comprehensive studies on nostalgia, its adaptive functions and effects on humans. A psychologist at the University of Surrey in England, Dr. Erica Hepper, discovered that nostalgia levels tend to rise among young adults, dip in middle age, then rise again during old age.[2]

I left my corporate job (yes, that "ultra-glamorous" job I loved so much) after having my second son and started a home-based business to continue my career and be more present at home. The stress of travel and long hours was disrupting our family. And the truth was, I didn't want to be on the road all the time and employ a full-time nanny. I wanted to be home with my boys. I wanted to be home when my boys woke up in the morning, and I wanted to be there to put them to bed at night. I wanted to make their lunch, put them down for naps, take them to their daily activities, music classes, and playdates.

There was "something" about the career I left behind that always had me thinking. I couldn't put my finger on exactly what it was, though I thought about it a lot. Years went by, and I was still romanticizing my corporate career. I thought about it so much that I decided to give it another shot. Five years after I left my corporate career, I received a job opportunity from a former colleague. In a fit of nostalgia, I took the job . . . and resigned sixty days later.

I learned the hard way: "**Don't make decisions based on nostalgia.**" It took me going back to that job to realize that I wasn't the same person anymore. What *once was* a romance was no longer a fit for me. That "something" I always thought about was just nostalgia.

Think about an experience or relationship that you've wrapped in nostalgia and ask yourself why you put it on a pedestal. Then, be brutally honest and write down three "truths" about the experience and why you might be holding on to it. Are you romanticizing the past, or is nostalgia telling you something you might be missing in your current life?

Use that information to help yourself evolve in your purpose, focus, and priorities.

Be who you CAME to be, not a copy of who you once were.

GET MENTALLY FIT

*Always remember you are braver
than you believe, stronger than you
seem, and smarter than you think.*

CHRISTOPHER ROBIN

GET MENTALLY FIT

A truth in life: what we believe we are worth is what we will GET in return.

What are you worth?
What is your time worth?
What is your work worth?

Positive thinking is powerful. Studies show that positive thinking directly impacts your success and even your health. Johns Hopkins expert Dr. Lisa R. Yanek and her colleagues discovered that people with a family history of heart disease who also had a positive outlook were one-third less likely to have a heart attack or other cardiovascular event within five to twenty-five years than those with a more negative outlook.[3] That's some heartwarming science!

In addition to the health benefits, positive thinking is directly correlated to your level of emotional intelligence. Emotional intelligence plays a direct role in our overall fulfillment, happiness, and success in life. Understanding my emotional intelligence, or EQ, has been a focus of mine since I was in my 20's. The study of EQ has been so fulfilling to me that in the Spring of 2019, I became a certified Emotional Intelligence Practitioner through Otto

Kroeger Associates. The EQ-i 2.0 Model in which I am certified in is comprised of sixteen specifically defined components of socio-emotional functioning, each of which plays a critical role in personal and professional effectiveness.

Your emotional intelligence can be measured through the EQ-i 2.0 assessment, and research shows that you can elevate and increase your emotional intelligence over time. I encourage you to get curious about your EQ and the opportunities to elevate it. In the meantime, I'm going to give you my personal definition of emotional intelligence. Emotional intelligence is understanding how you feel and then choosing how you show up. It's about being "mentally fit."

Being mentally fit is the capacity to recognize and understand your thoughts and emotions. And most importantly, recognize when your thoughts and self-limiting beliefs are holding you back. How you view yourself directly impacts how you show up daily. And how you show up directly impacts your success. If you don't believe you're worthy or capable of achieving your goals, you will NEVER achieve them.

Henry Ford said, "If you think you can, or you think you can't, you're right." Negative self-talk and assumed constraints will always exist. *We're only human.* It's natural to question our capability and worth. You are not your thoughts. It's not uncommon to have negative and self-limiting thoughts. When we are mentally fit, we understand that those are just thoughts, not truths. Being mentally fit will help you recognize when you are in a negative rut of self-doubt so you can flip the switch and change your internal narrative.

You have to believe in yourself beyond reason. *Yes,* you're capable, and *yes,* you're worthy of all of the success in the world. **How you view yourself is how you will show up. You are a magnet to whatever you truly believe.**

Your vibe attracts your tribe. The universe will present opportunity and success to match your self-worth and understanding of who you came to be. When you believe in your talent, ability, and self-worth, the universe rewards you with those qualities in return.

> HERE'S A SECRET
>
> *Yes, you're capable, and yes, you're worthy of all of the success in the world.*

When we live in fear and scarcity, we get fear and scarcity. When we live in a state of abundance, self-worth, and limitless success—we are rewarded with more of the same.

Get mentally fit. It will drastically change your overall life satisfaction and success. And here's a secret I know as a truth: life is just a helluva lot more fun with a positive daily outlook.

THE MOST IMPORTANT STORY

You can change your life by

changing the story you tell yourself.

KINDRA HALL

THE MOST IMPORTANT STORY

There are three types of stories:

1. The stories you tell others.

2. The stories you are told.

3. The stories you tell yourself.

The most important stories are the stories you tell yourself. There's no louder voice than the one in your head—it's also the voice you're most familiar with. Isn't it curious how we can talk ourselves into or out of almost anything? You might have heard the phrase "talking is legitimizing." In other words, say something enough times, and it sounds legitimate.

What are the conversations you have with yourself on a daily basis? What self-limiting stories have you told yourself so many times they FEEL like the truth? These stories are your *assumed constraints*. Assumed constraints are the lies we have told ourselves so many times they feel like our truths.

Ken Blanchard, world-renowned business consultant and author of *Self Leadership and the One Minute Manager* says, "An assumed constraint is a belief you have, based on past experience, that limits your current and future experiences."[4]

Blanchard shares a memorable story of a circus elephant. I always feel bad for baby elephants when I hear or share this example, but the illustration is powerful. "When they begin to train an elephant for the circus," says Blanchard, "they chain the baby elephant's leg to a pole in the ground. The baby elephant wants to get away. He pulls and tugs, but he can't escape—the chain is too big,

> HERE'S A SECRET
>
> *The most important stories are the stories you tell yourself.*

and the pole is too deep in the ground. So he stops trying. As he grows up, he just assumes he can't get away. Today he's a six-ton elephant. He could sneeze and pull out the chain—but he doesn't even try. Circus trainers say they can put a piece of string around that six-ton elephant's leg, and he won't break away."[5]

What in your life is causing you to act like the baby elephant? What assumed constraints are holding you back? What are you chained to that is keeping you from being who you came to be? These are the lies you might be telling yourself:

I'm not smart enough.
I'm not thin enough.
I'm not a leader.
I don't have enough time.

I don't have the money.

I'll never be good at that.

I wish I could, but...

A woman approached me after a keynote with tears in her eyes. She said, "I've never been called out on my assumed constraints before, and I've realized that I've used the fact that I'm a single mom as an excuse for way too long. The excuse has robbed me of joy, experiences, health, and love. I'm going to stop today." She went on to tell me that she's used it to avoid social situations, dating, applying for jobs, and even exercise, making excuses including: "I can't because I'm a single mom;" "If I wasn't a single mom, I could do that;" and, "That sounds like fun, but I can't because I'm a single mom."

We always make time for what's important to us. Are *you* important to you? If you're not, take steps toward the truth that you are important. Claim it! **No one is ever going to care more about your aspirations, hopes, and dreams than YOU. Start believing in yourself beyond reason. You're perfectly flawed and 100% authentic.** Give yourself grace in the process.

We get what we believe. If you tell yourself something enough times, you will start to believe it. Stop telling yourself lies. Stop making excuses. Be the VOICE of "I can and I will."

Be the AUTHENTIC voice of who you came to be. *Own it.*

PART

Three

LIVE IT

There is no passion to be found in

playing small - in settling for a life

that is less than the one you are

capable of living.

NELSON MANDELA

THE "F" WORD

I have learned over the years that

when one's mind is made up, this

diminishes fear; knowing what

must be done does away with fear.

ROSA PARKS

THE " F " WORD

Invitational fear: The fear you feel when you're dreaming bigger for yourself.

Invitational fear is the fear that arises when you desire to change because you want more for your life. Invitational fear causes your heart to pound, palms to sweat, breathing to race, and stomach to flip. You may experience unrealistic thoughts of failure and judgment. The fear can be so paralyzing that it causes you to retreat, take no action, and revert to your old self. You're consumed by thoughts of,

What if I fail?

What if it doesn't work out?

What will others think of me?

Am I capable of actually doing that?

I don't think I'm enough.

When you observe yourself saying these words to the mirror, recognize it as invitational fear and embrace it. Invitational fear is one of the first signs you're on the right track.

When was the last time you experienced this type of fear? If you haven't experienced invitational fear for a while, you're overdue: it is time to start dreaming a little bit bigger. You're ready for an uplevel.

> Uplevel: *a better, stronger, smarter, more confident, and authentic version of YOU.*

An uplevel is an intentional process of positive change. It requires you to make choices and decisions that will align you with who you came to be. Think of it as a video game. Once you master and conquer a certain level, you level up or experience an uplevel.

Uplevels and changes in our everyday routine and lifestyle are exciting. But quite often scary. The future, with all its uncertainty, is intimidating. When you feel afraid as you look into the future, it's because you **care deeply** about whatever it is you are dreaming about. *We don't get nervous, anxious, or fearful of things we don't care about. We experience invitational fear because we care and want more. And yes, you deserve more!*

HERE'S A SECRET

You're ready for an uplevel.

Be who you CAME to be. Who you came to be is not who you were, and that requires change. That requires YOU to change. You must act and move through the fear.

One of the most famous notions around "fear" is just to fight it with courage. Let's be REAL. It's one thing for someone to tell you to fight fear with courage. It's another to dig a little deeper, deploy ideas, resources, and tools to gain the confidence needed to muster up the courage to take action and fight fear.

So let's go. I've dedicated the entire last section of this book, Part Three, to help you move through fear, never play small again, and live the life you desire.

GOAL DIGGER

You can only become

truly accomplished at something you

love. Don't make money your goal.

Instead, pursue the things

you love doing, and then do them so

well that people can't take their eyes

off you.

MAYA ANGELOU

GOAL DIGGER

Goals. We all got 'em.

Get in shape.

Make more money.

Earn the promotion.

Run a marathon.

Write the book.

Start the business.

Take the class.

The statistics on Americans achieving goals is daunting. If you conduct an internet search on this topic, you'll find lots of studies on how many actually achieve their goals. The numbers I've found range from 3-8% of Americans who proclaim achievement of their annual goals. Experts claim these low numbers stem from not writing goals down, not sharing goals with family and friends, and not setting realistic goals.

I believe the main reason we don't achieve our goals is that we are not honest with ourselves about what we *want* and what we are willing to *work* for.

First things first: If your goals aren't "fulfilling" to you, abandon them immediately.

Why would you waste time and energy trying to achieve something that isn't fulfilling to you?

In Part One, I shared a lot about why fulfillment is energizing, sustainable, and creates epic moments of happiness and success. Your goals MUST be fulfilling, or you will NEVER achieve them. Sometimes we set goals because we think it's expected of us that we *should* do this or *should* achieve that.

I worked in the social selling/direct sales arena for ten years and I continue to keynote speak, train and consult with many direct sales companies.

QUICK RANT:

I like the direct sales industry. It gives women flexible entrepreneurship and the ability to design a life they love. The women I work with in this industry are joyful, fulfilled and genuinely enjoy their work. Most women become a representative for their company because they share a passion for the products, desire a flexible income and enjoy the community of supportive women. I'm here for it and I'm here for you. There are still naysayers who call these companies "pyramid schemes" and that is just not true. Today's savvy direct sales company is not a 1980s pyramid scheme. If direct sales is not for you and who you came to be, that's okay. But no need to throw shade on women who have found a passion and purpose in direct sales. Let her be who she came to be.

(whew....just had to make that little rant before we move onto goals).

Okay, back to goals. In direct sales, SMART goals (Specific, Measurable, Attainable, Relevant, Time-Bound) are the backbone of corporate and individual success. Any given company has specific goals that independent sales reps are encouraged (or required) to meet. And the higher they climb in sales and team building, the more they are financially rewarded.

The most successful and happiest reps align their personal goals (financial, recognition, lifestyle, etc.) with the various opportunities that exist at the company. For some, their goal is to make their "side-hustle" a full-time job. For others, they simply want a "side-hustle" to make a little extra money.

Not everyone in direct sales has the desire to build a six-figure business. Some representatives love sharing the product and just want a little extra spending money. And there are many who aren't money motivated, but they love the product and enjoy being part of a community of supportive women.

So why would a representative who is fulfilled by selling a little and being part of the community set a HUGE goal to hit a level in the compensation plan? The short answer is they thought they should because the company and other representatives hyped it up and told them how amazing it is to be promoted to the top of the compensation plan. And rightfully so! When they achieved that promotion, it felt incredibly fulfilling! They were motivated AND fulfilled by the work it took to arrive at that level.

In my ten years as a leader in direct sales, I saw about 20% of the sales team, company-wide, achieve the goals they "thought" they wanted or "should" try to hit. Yikes, a 20% success rate?! That is staggeringly low.

This is what happens when you set goals that aren't aligned with a purpose that fulfills you. This is what happens when you set goals for the wrong reasons and don't want to put in the WORK required to hit the goal. The reason only 20% achieved the goal is because only 20% actually desired to achieve the goal. The other 80% put the goal out there because they thought it was what they *should* pursue. The lack of desire to put in the work made the goal unachievable and ultimately undesirable.

The worst part about setting goals that you don't want is that instead of feeling accomplished, you end up feeling deflated. You feel small and perhaps even ashamed for not hitting the goal.

Who cares what anyone else THINKS you should do. Set goals that are important to YOU. Achieving YOUR personal goals is where you'll find fulfillment. And that fulfillment will drive your work ethic.

BOTTOM LINE: don't set goals for things you don't truly want. Set goals that align with what is fulfilling to you.

THERE'S SOMETHING ABOUT "THAT BAG"

My life changed the day I moved

beyond just wishing for things,

and I started earning them. That is

the day I learned that we don't get

what we wish for, we get what we

work for.

STEVE MARABOLI

THERE'S SOMETHING
ABOUT "THAT BAG"

Shortly after I got out of college, I wanted a Louis Vuitton bag. There was something about that bag. The brown and beige designer print, leather handles with a dash of red, and beautiful gold hardware. I was obsessed with the brand and the bag.

But let me be clear, I was twenty-four years old, and a Louis Vuitton wasn't anywhere in my near future. At the time, my husband and I were broke. We were newlyweds and had debt from college and our wedding. We were working hard to pay off our debt and agreed not to have unnecessary expenses. (Yes, unfortunately, a Louis Vuitton would have fallen under an unnecessary expense. *Insert eye roll by twenty-four-year-old me.)*

So like any wishful and smart "Daddy's girl," I decided I would plant a seed with my dad about my desire for a Louis Vuitton, thinking maybe he would splurge for Christmas and get me one! Well, guess what? He didn't get me one for Christmas. In fact, he didn't understand why I was obsessed with this bag. Just like my husband, he thought the price tag was outrageous. "Why on earth would anyone spend that kind of money on a purse?" he asked me.

But, just as I thought, he wasn't the type of dad who liked to let down his little girl. A few months after Christmas, he was in NYC and snagged a "really nice" Louis Vuitton. The only problem was that it was fake *(insert eye roll by twenty-five-year-old me)*.

But I had to give it to him, he was so excited to give me "the bag." He thought he made the score of the century. He told me it looked *just* like the ones he saw in the NYC Louis Vuitton store and that he was able to find it on the street for a fraction of the price.

I didn't want to disappoint him, so I tried to carry it, but it just didn't feel right. I knew it wasn't the "real" thing. I felt like a fake every time I carried it. It felt like I was trying to be someone I wasn't yet.

So I set a REALLY BIG goal for myself. I set a goal to pay off ALL our debt. Once I did that, I would buy the Louis Vuitton I always dreamed of.

Shortly after I set this goal, I landed my dream sales job. I decided that if I exceeded my targets, my quarterly bonuses would allow me to pay off our debt in a year. And then I could finally buy "the bag." I got to work. I kicked ass at my job. And within a year, I paid off our debt.

It was time to buy my first Louis Vuitton. I got online and browsed bag after bag until I settled on a bigger bag that I could carry for work. It had perfect structure and was everything I had dreamed of. So I did it. I ordered my very first Louis Vuitton! Two days later, the bag came in the mail. I was so excited to open the box; I was literally trembling. (We didn't then and still don't have a Louis Vuitton store in Kansas City. *Insert eye roll by forty-four-year-old me.*)

I proudly admired and carefully opened the beautiful brown box that had a hot pink satin ribbon tied around it. Inside the box was the Louis Vuitton dust bag, and inside the dust bag was the gorgeous Louis Vuitton bag I had always dreamed of owning. I felt nervous and a little anxious, thinking maybe I shouldn't have the bag or keep the bag or even carry the bag. *Was it too flashy? Was it out of my league? Maybe this was still an irresponsible purchase?*

As I contemplated returning the Louis Vuitton bag, I packed it up and put it back into the box. It was at this exact moment Jason, my sales manager, came into my office. Jason knew I had wanted this bag for a very long time. We talked about it during our one-on-one strategy meetings. He knew about my goal to crush my sales numbers, pay off debt, and buy the bag of my dreams. *"What are you doing?"* he asked. I told him, *"I think I'm going to send this bag back. It just seems like too much, and maybe I shouldn't have bought it."*

Jason paused, looked at me, and said, *"Here's what you're going to do. You're going to put all of your shit in that bag, and I'm taking you out to lunch. We're going to set new goals for you to crush*

I

earned

THAT

DAMN

BAG!

so you can buy a designer bag every quarter if you want. Tara, YOU
EARNED THAT BAG!"

And so I did. I put all of my shit in the bag, and off to lunch
we went. We set bigger goals, and I continued to kick ass in my job.
And yes, I continued to buy more Louis Vuitton handbags.

I carried the bag with my head held high. I carried it with confidence. I carried it because I EARNED THAT DAMN BAG!

Something magical happened when I set this big goal for myself. When I believed in myself and worked tirelessly to exceed my
goals and reward myself for my achievements, everything started
leveling up. I stopped playing small and was promoted several
times in the coming years.

I carried my first Louis Vuitton so much I had to have new
handles put on it. I still have it and still carry it occasionally. If you
visit my office, you'll see it sitting on the top shelf of my bookcase.
My desk faces the shelves, and I admire the bag every day. At first, I
was worried it looked too flashy to sit on an office bookshelf. And
then I reminded myself what it stood for. This wasn't just a "designer bag" but a symbol representing the first time in my life I believed
in myself and put in the work to crush a big goal.

The bag is a reminder that I can achieve and earn ANY-
THING I am willing to WORK FOR. It's a reminder for me to
set goals and go all-in on me; it is a reminder to show up confidently and never play small. It is a reminder to be who I came to be.

Tyrese Gibson once said, "The dream is free. The hustle is sold separately."

Whatever you want, you *can* achieve. You just have to dream big, believe in yourself, and put in the work.

Trust me; you're worth it.

BUTTERFLY GOALS

Always be braver than

your butterflies.

AMANDA THOMPSON

BUTTERFLY GOALS

A caterpillar didn't come to be a caterpillar; it came to be a butterfly. Who did you come to be?

Let's talk about BUTTERFLY GOALS. These goals are big, wild, ambitious, extraordinary, and maybe even unimaginable.

What would you accomplish if you could do ANYTHING in the world? Yes, anything. This goal might be so big, so wild, and so crazy you've never thought about it. Until now. I'm sure a big goal just crept into your mind. Perhaps it was so big that you immediately extinguished the thought.

Light it back up! Let's go! It's time to manifest your butterfly goal.

Before a butterfly is a butterfly, it is a caterpillar—a big, fat, hairy, and slow CATERPILLAR. And what happens to a big, fat, hairy, slow caterpillar? Even a child knows the answer to this. It becomes a beautiful, brilliant BUTTERFLY.

Right now, you might resonate with caterpillar status, and butterfly status might seem almost impossible. But it is not. The butterfly has one of the most fascinating life cycles of all creatures. A butterfly emerges out of the metamorphosis of a caterpillar. If you didn't know the science behind this transformation, you might deem it impossible. But as you do know, it is 100% POSSIBLE. A caterpillar becomes a butterfly through a challenging, difficult, timely, and beautiful transformation.

Just as the caterpillar did not come into this world to remain a caterpillar, you did not come into this world to remain what you have been but to become who you came to be. Just like the possibility of the metamorphosis of a caterpillar to a butterfly, YOU are possible.

Like metamorphosis, butterfly goals are a process that takes TIME. And they take as much time as they take. Some caterpillars complete metamorphosis in a few weeks, others a few months, and some even a few years. But **the caterpillar is DESTINED to be a butterfly. It's who it came to be.**

The little caterpillar who eats and dreams of butterfly days one day stops eating and realizes, "It's time." (For all the *The Very Hungry Caterpillar* by Eric Carle reading moms out there, you know how it goes.) The caterpillar crawls up a branch and forms a chrysalis. During its time in the chrysalis, it completely deconstructs itself, reinvents itself, and emerges as a butterfly.

Take a moment and write it down,

My Butterfly Goal _____

_____

Why is this important to me?

_____

_____

_____

_____

_____

_____

_____

_____

_____

Why do I want to achieve it?

_____

_____

_____

_____

_____

_____

_____

_____

When you focus on big butterfly goals instead of small daily goals, you'll be surprised at the growth and change that occurs, even just one day at a time. By focusing on your BIG butterfly goal, your daily goals will become clear, aligned, and fulfilling. Opportunities will present themselves, and you will slowly work toward beautiful butterfly wings.

The caterpillar is DESTINED to be a butterfly. It's who it came to be.

Later in the book, I share the story of my childhood dream to be on a game show. This is just one example of a butterfly goal in my life. It took most of my life to achieve it, but I did it! I was on ABC's $100,000 Pyramid in 2018. And if I can achieve a wild butterfly goal like getting on a national game show, you can achieve your butterfly goal too.

My grandmother gave me a college graduation gift that I still cherish. It was a simple gift that has stood the test of time. In fact, the gift still sits on my office bookshelf. It's a metal frame with an angel and a Paul Meyer quote: "Whatever you vividly imagine, ardently desire, sincerely believe, and enthusiastically act upon . . . must inevitably come to pass."

So, are you ready to imagine your butterfly goal? Desire it? Believe in it? Share it? And enthusiastically wiggle toward it?

Go ahead. Write it down and let the metamorphosis and manifestation begin.

RISKY BUSINESS

---

*Take chances, make mistakes. That's
how you grow. Pain nourishes your
courage. You have to fail in order to
practice being brave.*

MARY TYLER MOORE

RISKY BUSINESS

Because we have the capacity to plan, dream, and hope for the future, we also have the ability to be consumed by fear.

What if it doesn't work out?

What if I lose money?

What if no one likes it?

What will others think?

What if I fail?

What if all of the above happens?

My grandmother once told me, *"It's only a mistake if it happens twice. The first time is a lesson you need to learn."* She told me this when I was in my early 20s, down on my luck, and wondering about the next steps in life. And isn't it curious I have NO REC-OLLECTION of what I was fretting about? I only remember her advice.

"It's only a mistake if it happens twice. The first time is a lesson you need to learn."

I ran with it; I ran fast and hard with those words. And I have learned a lot of "lessons" in the process. I've used this single piece of advice as a permission slip to take all the calculated risks. If I wasn't going to fail, what did I have to lose? If I no longer thought of risks with a negative consequence, what could I achieve?

There is a question we've all heard tossed around: "What would you do if you knew you wouldn't fail?"

I promise you, you won't FAIL. It's only a failure if you make the same mistake twice. You'll make mistakes, you'll learn lessons along the way, and you will continue to get BETTER.

One of the biggest lessons I've learned along the way is this: Did it work out as I thought? NEVER. Did it work out? AL-WAYS. My hope is that you find that *when things don't work out, they actually do.*

Fear of failure is an unrealistic expectation that we won't have adversity or setbacks. Expect adversity. Expect setbacks. Expect mistakes. Expect hard times. Expect plan A to end up as plan Z. *It will be messy. It will be challenging. It will be FULFILLING.*

Give yourself permission to FAIL. **We have to stop looking at failures as a failure and start looking at failures as PROGRESS.**

I promise you this: you'll never regret going all-in on who you came to be. You can play it small and play it safe, but you'll never step into who you came to be until you start taking the RISKS necessary to level up. You have to learn and implement those lessons.

So now I'm telling YOU, *"It's only a mistake if it happens twice. The first time was just a lesson you need to learn."*

So there you have it. Learn the lessons. Take risks. Run.

DECONSTRUCT FEAR

Risk comes from not knowing what

you're doing.

WARREN BUFFETT

DECONSTRUCT FEAR

FEAR. *Fear* of failure, *fear* of not being good enough, *fear* of financial loss, *fear* of commitment, and a *fear* of change are all paralyzing. And the platitudes we hear just don't help: *Feel the fear and do it anyway; Fight fear with courage; Fear is nothing more than a state of mind; Just jump.*

The quotes on fear are endless. And sayings like, "Feel the fear and do it anyway," look great on paper. But psychologically, the fear can still paralyze you. I love a great motivational quote as much as the next person, but sometimes we need more "proof" than just a quote telling us to jump.

So how do you get the proof? *I have a secret . . . and of course I'm going to share it with you.* A pen, paper, and your honest, vulnerable self are all you need to decide if it's worth leaning into that fear. Here is a great exercise that can help you face and walk through your fear. On page 160-161 you wrote down your BIG BUTTERFLY GOAL; why it's so important to you and why you want to achieve it. Now on the next page, write down all of the RISKS that are involved with this goal. When we can name our FEAR and the RISKS, we can conquer that fear. More often than not, what we fear is not failure itself but all of the RISKS we are

The risks!

_____

_____

_____

_____

_____

_____

_____

_____

_____

_____

_____ *My fears...*

_____

_____

_____

_____

_____

_____

_____

_____

taking. If you can deconstruct the fear by naming the risks, you will find the courage to conquer it.

Risks ignite fear. What's incredible about the process of deconstructing fear by naming the risks is that it settles the emotions and organizes your thoughts to help you make big decisions. You can take this a step further and ask, "What if I don't do XYZ?" Often, the fear of regret is worse than the fear of the unknown.

> HERE'S A SECRET
>
> *Often, the fear of regret is worse than the fear of the unknown.*

Once we name the risks, we usually see that we are worth it. We are worth taking all the risks. And then, we can move into a big decision with confidence instead of fear.

Let me tell you a story about how my husband and I used this method to make a HUGE jump.

Scott graduated from The University of Kansas with two degrees: Business and Chemical Engineering. (Yes, he's the guy you want on your Trivial Pursuit team.) After college, he landed a job at a Kansas City engineering firm. It was a job he really enjoyed. After working there for a few years, he decided to pursue his Master's Degree in Business. Like many firms, one of the perks for the engineers was they would pay for your MBA if you stayed at the company for several years after you completed your degree.

For two years, Scott went to night school. During this time, he developed a passion for investments. One of the highlights of his MBA was getting to present an investment idea to Warren Buffet. Although he enjoyed his current career as an engineer, his interest in investments was strong enough that he started exploring job opportunities at local mutual fund companies. What he quickly learned was that this was an extremely competitive industry. Even the Kansas City-based mutual fund companies did the majority of their recruiting from Ivy League MBA programs. But his passion fueled his tenacity to keep looking for an opportunity.

Scott learned of an internship program at a local investment firm—a promising lead. It was a twelve-week, paid summer internship. The program was designed to recruit Ivy League students. It brought them to Kansas City for a summer so they would fall in love with the city and company and move to K.C. upon completion of their degree.

Scott was invited to interview for the internship and nailed it! He was offered a summer internship with one of the investment teams. And now he had a decision to make, one that came with lots of fear. The fear was real because there were a lot of risks. And the risks were high.

> » *He would have to resign from his current job at the time.*

> » *He would have to pay back his MBA to the company.*

» *The job was only twelve weeks, with no guarantee of a permanent position.*

» *What if he didn't like the program?*

» *What if he didn't like the team?*

» *What if he found himself unemployed after twelve weeks?*

» *What would family and friends think about this?*

» *What if he didn't take it? Would he be miserable? Resentful? Would he regret this?*

Those were big life-changing risks. Ultimately, he had two options:

1. Play small and stay at his current job.

2. Follow his passion and purpose and live the life he desired.

The rewards of following his passion and doing fulfilling life work outweighed ANY risk. So, he did it: he resigned from his job, paid back his MBA, and took the twelve-week internship. He was offered a permanent position after the internship. Fast forward sixteen years, and he's still working at the company and loves it.

Next time you find yourself in "fear mode" and wondering if you should take the first step toward your butterfly goal, deconstruct the fear by understanding the risks. And don't forget to add the risk of regret. Will you regret not going all-in on your butterfly goal? My mentor and friend, Dan Schoepf, often reminds me,

"There are two pains in life; the pain of discipline and the pain of regret." In three years, will you regret not starting today? Is the fear of regret stronger than the fear of discipline and the unknown? Once you understand the fear, risks, and regrets, I bet you'll discover you're worth the risk and ready to confidently lean into that fear and put in the time and discipline to achieve the goal.

I think you're worth big risks. I really do. You should too. You are enough. Deconstruct risk, fight fear, act courageously and confidently to be who you came to be.

Life is too short to play small and safe.

MIRROR MIRROR ON THE WALL

There is only one corner of the

universe you can be certain of

improving, and that's your own self.

ALDOUS HUXLEY

MIRROR MIRROR ON THE WALL

One of the best personal development skills you can learn is the ability to self-assess. As we get older, we rarely receive feedback on performance, ability, and opportunities for growth. And let's face it, we often don't want to receive or desire to hear others' opinions. This is why the ability to self-assess accurately is key.

No one teaches this essential skill that's required for growth. It's not a part of any common education system. Therefore, it's also one of the biggest problems facing our youth. Today's youth have no idea how to self-assess. They are stunted in their growth toward being able to assess and improve their skill sets because they are all too often showered with praise and participation trophies.

Corporate America calls this process of self-assessment a SWOT analysis (Strengths, Weakness, Opportunity, and Threat). I call it using "a clear mirror to self-assess." A "clear mirror" is a term that was commonly cited during my time at Careerbuilder.com, and it's stuck with me since.

What happens when you're looking in a mirror? You focus on yourself. You're not concerned with what's going on in the back-ground—you're 100% focused on you. **Ultimately, the only thing** you can control is you. How you show up, how you act, how you react, what you decide to celebrate, and what you decide to work on. You focus on YOU.

HERE'S A SECRET

Ultimately, the only thing you can control is you.

I've been working with my boys on using a clear mirror to help them self-assess. It's really simple. Let's dig into this a little bit.

What is the first thing your child says when they come running to you after a game or event? They often say, "How did I do?" And what is the response you often give? "You were GREAT! You were AWESOME! WOW. I'm so proud of you! Let's go celebrate with some ice cream!"

Parents generally tell children how amazing they are and how proud of them they are. Now, I'm not recommending you come at them with constant criticism, but I *am* recommending an opportunity for self-assessment. Next time they ask you, "How did I do, Mom?" Instead of telling them about their epic greatness, respond with a big encouraging smile and ask them, "How do *you* think you did?"

When I first started asking this question to my son, Ben, he'd say, "I was pretty awesome." (After all, I had been telling him that for quite a while.) Instead of continuing to shower him with compliments, I'd simply respond by saying, "You had some shining moments, especially that pop-fly you caught in the bottom of the fifth inning. But let's talk about when you were in the batter's box at the bottom of the third inning."

"That pitcher was terrible, wasn't he, Mom?"

"I'm not talking about the pitcher; I'm talking about you. How did *you* do in the batter's box?"

"Well, I swung at a pitch that was too high. But that umpire didn't know where the strike zone was."

"I'm not talking about the umpire; I'm talking about *you*."

"Yeah, I just got under it and didn't hit it in the sweet spot."

Over time, Ben used this "clear mirror" to self-assess his performance and understand what he was doing well and what he needed to work on. In other words, the clear mirror provided opportunities for improvement. It lit a fire in him to get better. He started asking for lessons and extra practice time to level up his skills.

It's been years since Ben started self-assessing. He's a teenager now and never asks, "How did I do?" He doesn't have to ask me because he knows how he did. Now, we just talk about the game, where he shined, and what he needs to work on. He's become a good athlete, has a great attitude, is a humble winner, and is not a sore loser.

Give it a shot. Next time you get the opportunity to answer the question "How did I do?" reply with "How do you think you did?"

And the next time you want to ask someone, "How did I do?" make sure you've checked yourself in a clear mirror to self-assess.

POST YOUR SELFIE

The most alluring thing a woman

can have is confidence.

BEYONCE KNOWLES

POST YOUR SELFIE

Why do we play small when it comes to sharing our strengths, passions, and things we are GOOD at? Shine light on your strengths and passions.

Post your selfie.

Share your workout.

Talk about your business.

Celebrate your side hustle

Photoshoot your cooking.

Tell us about your makeup techniques.

Brag on your kids.

If you like it—SHARE IT.

When someone says to you: "Wow, you look beautiful," learn to say, "Thank You. You just made me *feel* beautiful."

We must celebrate our strengths. When we downplay the things we love, we can't step into our authenticity. You didn't come to shine a dull light—you came to shine a bright light! You can show up perfectly flawed and confident. There is a big difference between being arrogant and being confident.

Someone who is arrogant believes they are better than others. They tear others down to build themselves up. They don't give compliments or lift others. They are not kind or empathetic.

Confidence is being perfectly flawed and shining your light. You know your strengths and show up authentic to who you came to be. You believe in yourself and in others. You give and accept compliments genuinely. You're empathic and assertive, optimistic and realistic. You are independent and have incredible interpersonal relationships.

You have NO REASON not to show up every day with confidence. There is only ONE YOU. You were born perfectly flawed with purpose and passions.

Consider the phrase, "Perception is reality." How do you perceive yourself?

Once you start perceiving yourself as a worthy, beautiful, capable, smart, intelligent, authentic, and CONFIDENT woman . . . you will become her.

Start today. Show up as who you came to be. Shine your light!

PUSHING THE LIMITS

Limits like fears are often

just an illusion.

MICHAEL JORDAN

PUSHING THE LIMITS

Limitations are often misunderstood as weaknesses. Limitations are circumstantial. Limitations can change—they ebb and flow. But you need to know they are *not* weaknesses. It's essential for you to identify your limitations so you can set appropriate timelines for your big butterfly goals.

Limitations are also NOT EXCUSES. Check yourself. Are you using a limitation as an excuse? If so, just stop. Excuses only sound good to those who are making them.

> HERE'S A SECRET
>
> *Excuses only sound good to those who are making them.*

Let's say that you want to exercise five days a week. (Great goal. You got this!) Your limitation is that you have two small children, and your gym doesn't have childcare. Those two things are going to limit you, but they are not going to stop you or hold you back; they will just limit when you can exercise. So now you must find a WAY to work around the limitations.

You could exercise early in the morning, late in the day, or when you have childcare.

You could find a new gym that accepts childcare.

You could invest in a double stroller and take your kids with you on long walks/runs.

You could find a way to do in-home workouts when the children are sleeping.

You could download the Peloton app and work out from home.

No, that isn't a paid Peloton sponsorship *(I wish)*. And no, you don't need the Peloton bike or treadmill. You can participate in the Peloton app workouts from anywhere. They have everything from outdoor workouts to yoga to bike to strength-training to boot-camps. Yes, this was a life-changing secret I discovered when my workouts were limited during the pandemic, and now I'm sharing it with you!

So YES, you are limited, but NO, you are not defeated.

Take a minute and think about a goal you are working toward? What is currently limiting you? Are you using the limitation as an EXCUSE or finding a way to work around the limitation? If you are using it as an excuse, it's time to shift the narrative. How can you work around that limitation vs. using it as an excuse for not achieving your goal?

Sometimes limitations will require you to adjust the TIME-LINE of your goals. Notice the large print there—the TIME-

yes

YOU

ARE

LIMITED

BUT

not

DEFEATED

LINE. Pursue your goals, just with an attainable and measurable timeline.

For instance, you want to get certified as a nutritionist so you can monetize your passion for health and wellness. Currently, you work an full-time job. That's a limitation. You won't be able to take nutrition classes during the day; you'll have to take them at night. So instead of the certification taking six months to complete, it's going to take a year. That's not a bad thing! It doesn't make you less because it's taking you longer. It is honoring your current situation and STILL going all-in on being who you came to be.

Whether it takes six months, a year, or five years, START TODAY. Trust me, a year from now, you will wish you started the day you read this book.

The bottom line is that time is on the move, and it takes as long as it takes to achieve your goals. Don't ever let a limitation keep you from being who you came to be.

PS. You're worth *all* the time it takes to work around those limitations.

THE $100,000 BUTTERFLY GOAL

I always thought that common sense would prevail. But on a game show, there is no common sense.

WAYNE BRADY

THE $100,000 BUTTERFLY GOAL

Growing up, my biggest dream was to be a contestant on a game show. I grew up in the '80s, when game shows ruled every television network. *Wheel of Fortune, Price is Right, $25,000 Pyramid, Family Feud, Press Your Luck, Let's Make a Deal, Win, Lose, or Draw.* Did I miss your favorite show?'

Around the age of ten, I declared my first butterfly goal: "I'm going to be on a game show," I told my two older brothers. They looked at me like I was nuts. "Tara," one retorted, "nobody from Courtland, Kansas is going to get on a game show. You'd have to live in New York or California to be on a game show."

I responded to many of their doubts with a determined glare (to this day, they know the look well); it's a look of "Just watch me —I'm gonna be on a damn game show!"

Years went by, and the dream slowly faded. There was a time in my mid-20s that I considered applying for *The Apprentice*. But those contestants had to leave their jobs and risk getting "You're Fired" by Donald Trump on national television. I loved my job and couldn't imagine living in an apartment with strangers for three months. I passed on applying.

More years went by. The dream I declared in 1989 faded into the abyss of time as the calendar flipped to 1999 and to 2009.

Nearly thirty years after that original butterfly goal, during an afternoon coffee meeting, I got my first real lead to landing a spot on a game show. I had recently been introduced to Rich, a fellow Kansas Citian and keynote speaker. Since we had so many of the same goals and mutual connections, we met for coffee to discuss business, life, goals, and achievements. Somewhere in the conversation, I mentioned, "One day, I'm gonna be on a game show."

"What?" Rich said, "I was on ABC's *$100,000 Pyramid* last year. And they recently emailed me to see if I knew anyone who might be a good fit." "No way!" I exclaimed, "Wow, that's so cool they asked you!" *Let's be real; I think it probably sounded more like,* "MEEEE! MEEE!! PLEASE PICK ME!!!"

He connected me to the casting agency, and after three months of grueling interviews, casting calls, gameplay, and background checks, my childhood dream came true: I was cast on ABCs Game Show, *$100,000 Pyramid*.

Here's the story of my game show experience. To be specific: Season Three, Episode Three of *$100,000 Pyramid*.

This word association game, inspired by the Bob Stewart-hosted 1973 gameshow, has two celebrities and their "average-joe" partners face off for a place in the Winner's Circle and a shot at **$100,000.** If you win the first two rounds, you win NOTHING except a trip to the Winner's Circle. However, once in the Winner's Circle, you have an opportunity to win $50,000. And if you get to the Winner's Circle a second time, you can win $100,000 (for a possible total of $150,000).

My celebrity pairing was two actors from *The Good Doctor*: Nicholas Gonzalez and Richard Schiff. They took turns as my game partner.

During the first round of the game, I played with Nicholas. I was the clue-giver, and he was the clue-guesser. And to put it lightly, I was tragic. I hadn't settled in, and he only answered a few of my clues correctly. I sensed he was annoyed and disappointed in my gameplay. And let's be real, so was I! But I kept my cool, collected my thoughts, and got dialed into the game. And then it happened; I took a couple of deep breaths, and boom, we found our stride, started working as a team, and earned a spot in the Winner's Circle. This was it; I was playing for $50,000!

My biggest childhood butterfly goal was becoming a reality. Not only did I make it ON the game show, but I also had the opportunity to WIN BIG!

Unfortunately, my trip to the Winner's Circle ignited my biggest fear: the fear of saying something STUPID on national television for all of America to hear. And yep, I did that. I made SUCH an embarrassing mistake.

For the clue "Famous Astronauts," I calmly and confidently

said, "Lance Armstrong." Nicholas immediately replied with "cy-clists, athletes," and I knew I had said the WRONG Armstrong.

I quickly said, "Pass!" on the "Famous Astronauts" category to immediately nail the next question: "Things That are Refreshing," with one solid clue of "Ice Cold Lemonade." Because of my blunder, I missed out on the $50,000, but I did end up with $12,500.

Not what I wanted, but not bad! If you hit a $12,500 jackpot on a slot machine in Vegas, you'd be pretty damn excited. But I wasn't excited. I was bummed. I was embarrassed. I was flustered. I felt so SILLY! How could I mix-up my Armstrongs! And how could I make such a silly mistake on national television that cost me over $35,000?

After the round, Michael Strahan, the show's host, walked over to me and asked me on national TV, "Tara, did you think he was going to ride his bike to the moon?" "I lost all my astronauts!" I said, laughing through the embarrassment.

On a bright note, I had prepared for this. I was mentally fit and had prepared enough to remind myself that I didn't have time to dwell on mistakes. I had a brief, five-minute break to refocus before I had a chance to get back in the Winner's Circle for a shot at $100,000.

In the next round, I played with Richard Schiff. We made a good team and got into a great rhythm. And you guessed it, we got back to the Winner's Circle. This time I had the opportunity to take home $100,000. Yes, I was playing for a six-figure grand prize, but more importantly, I was playing for redemption. As much as I wanted to win the money, I wanted to win so no one would remember the silly Armstrong snafu.

I knocked down one category after another and had over ten seconds to spare for the final category. But when the category was revealed, I was stumped.

"Types of Booths."

"A phone . . . A phone . . . A phone," I repeated and urged him on, but he wasn't getting it.

"A phone . . . A phone . . . A phone." Finally, another booth popped into my head.

"A voting." I switched up the clue.

"Booths," he said, "Types of Booths!"

The sirens started, confetti fell, and I won $100,000. If you include the first Winner's Circle round, the total was $112,500.

The moments after I won big are a blur. I signed papers that swore secrecy among friends and family and was escorted out of the studio. My Mom and husband were in the audience that day; they were also legally obligated to secrecy. We all left that studio in silence, with zero emotion and with an incredibly fun secret.

We sat quietly during a ten-minute cab ride to the hotel. We refrained from eye contact as we thought the cab driver would know. The secret was already burning inside! We stopped by the hotel bar, bought the best bottle of champagne they had, rushed to our room, jumped on the bed (yes, we did) and partied in an "OMG; WE JUST WON $112,500" celebration.

Months went by before the show aired. It felt like an eternity. We honored our contract of secrecy and silence and didn't tell anyone the outcome of the show—not even our boys. I mean, let's face it. If we had told them, the cat would have gotten out of the bag for sure. Little kids aren't the best secret-keepers.

As time passed, winning felt different. The joy and excitement of winning turned into anxiety. We went back and forth on whether or not to have a party or if we should just lay low. It was a lot of money, and I didn't want to come across as bragging, but I also wanted to shine light on this dream come true.

After a one-hour "therapy" session with my life coach, I decided to host a small party. And this gathering with family and close friends was one of the best nights of my adult life. I got to tell my childhood story and how my dream became a reality, how my original butterfly goal came true.

I was reminded that *it's okay to celebrate our WINS,* and if the people closest to you are really YOUR PEOPLE, they'll enjoy celebrating *your* wins just as much as their own wins. When you grasp that reality, you'll understand that dishing out celebration actually becomes more rewarding than receiving it. I'm grateful for a butterfly goal and a $100k Pyramid that unlocked such a pivotal secret in life.

PS. I'll celebrate YOU any day!

WHEN OPPORTUNITY KNOCKS

Investing in yourself is the best

investment you will ever make. It

will not only improve your life, it

will improve the lives of all those

around you.

ROBIN SHARMA

SECRET THIRTY-FOUR

WHEN OPPORTUNITY KNOCKS

Definition of opportunity

1: a favorable juncture of circumstances

2: a good chance for advancement or progress

We all have natural abilities, talents, gifts, and strengths. These are your "opportunities." These opportunities provide a favorable juncture of circumstances and a good chance for uplevels and success. Most likely, your opportunities align with your passion and purpose. Your opportunities are who you came to be. But if you don't recognize and invest in your opportunities, little advancement or progress will occur. It's not enough to rely on your God-given talents: you must invest in your talents and opportunities.

Professional athletes are a perfect example of recognizing and investing in their talent and opportunities. Most likely, they had natural athletic abilities from a young age. They realized they were "good" at a certain sport, and they enjoyed playing it. So they started investing their time, energy, and training to get better at their sport. They didn't just show up for the games and kick-ass; they worked tirelessly behind the scenes so they could show up at the game as the very best version of themselves. Athletes train, practice, stay late, rise early, watch films, and hire trainers to BE WHO THEY CAME TO BE. They know that the more they train and invest in their talents, the better they will get.

I'm curious why so many Americans don't hesitate to spend hundreds of dollars on a nice dinner and drinks, but when it comes to investing money for an online course, conference ticket, personal training session, or accountability coach, a common response is "It's not worth it."

Trust me: It's worth it; you're worth it.

HERE'S A SECRET

YOU will always be your best investment. No one cares more about your opportunities than YOU. You must be willing to invest in yourself.

YOU will always be your best investment. No one cares more about your opportunities than YOU. You must be willing to invest in yourself.

I spent YEARS trying to write this book before I hired a professional editor to hold me accountable and help me put the book together. When I invested in myself, my writing, and my time, I was able to find accountability as a means to publish this book in a matter of months—from writing the first word to holding the published book in my hands.

What are your God-given talents and opportunities? What would happen if you invested more time and training to elevate those opportunities?

I'm telling you: It would change the speed and trajectory of your success.

Take the class.

Hire the trainer.

Buy the book.

Go to the conference.

Invest in the business.

Put in the extra time.

Rise early.

Stay late.

You are WORTH IT. Your opportunities are who you came to be. When opportunity knocks, open the door and look in the mirror: you will be glad you did.

SEEING

IS

BELIEVING

Having a mental snapshot of where

you are, where you are going, and

what you are moving toward is

incredibly powerful.

SARA BLAKELY

SEEING IS BELIEVING

Hopefully, after the last chapter, you understand your opportunities and are ready to invest in you. Now it's time to VISUALIZE your success. It's time for you to self-actualize and BE WHO YOU CAME TO BE.

Self-actualization is the complete realization of one's potential and the full development of one's abilities and appreciation for life. This concept is at the top of the Maslow hierarchy of needs, so not every human being reaches it, *But YOU can.*

My grandmother told me that it's not enough to want something—you have to visualize yourself in the winning moment. So let's do it. Take some time and visualize who you came to be.

Get a strong visualization of who you came to be, and you will start to see your full potential.

Where are you?

How old are you?

Who is with you?

What are you wearing?

What are the smells?

How do you feel?

Where are you living?

How much money are you making?
What does your day look like?

There is incredible power in creating a strong visualization for what you desire. I love reading stories from Olympians who credit the power of visualization as a strategic training tactic that aided them to win the silver, gold or bronze medal. I'm definitely not an Olympic athlete, but I used the power of visualization to write and publish this book.

Once I had an honest and strong visualization of what I wanted for my book, I was able to really get cranking on it. I could see what I wanted the book to look like, feel like, read like, and then the words started flowing, the content poured, and the book started coming together. While I was writing, I started visualizing people reading the book. I'd see "her" reading the book and start to wonder,

How did she find out about the book?
Where did she buy the book?
Why did she buy my book?
What sections would she highlight or circle?
What would cause her pause and reflection?
Who would she buy a copy for?
Where would she keep the book?

I envisioned sharing my book on my social media stories. I visualized myself talking at conferences and virtual seminars and sharing my book with attendees. I closed my eyes and saw women reading this book and designing a life they love. This message would change how they show up. This book would help them believe in themselves and invest in their talents. This message would help them hold their head high with confidence and know they're worth any risk. My book would help them be who they came to be.

As I write these words, I'm close to the printing and publishing process. This is one of the last sections of the book I wrote. While writing this, I'm visualizing a book launch party—a party where I will celebrate the publication of my first book with friends and family.

And while I was writing this section, the strongest visualization happened: I could SMELL and FEEL the book. I closed my eyes, and I took in the smell of the freshly printed book. I felt the book in my hands, and I even heard the sound a book makes when you open a hardcover book for the first time. The crystal-clear visualization made my heart race with excitement, my eyes welled with tears of joy, and I felt incredibly humbled and proud of myself. I did it: I published a book.

I used the power of visualization and self-actualization to see, touch, and even smell this book coming to life. And now you're reading it. So I ask you, what are you going to bring to life? What are you going to visualize so clearly that it becomes your reality?

Start NOW. A strong visualization is how you self-actualize and be who you CAME to be.

BE BOLD.
BE CONFIDENT.
BE YOU.

If you're presenting yourself with

confidence, you can pull off pretty

much anything.

KATY PERRY

BE BOLD.
BE CONFIDENT.
BE YOU.

Confident women are magnetically drawn to success. They attract opportunities. They elevate the vibe of a room and empower other women to believe they're worth it too.

Earlier in the book, I wrote, *"What we believe we're worth is what we'll get in return."*

In other words, our thoughts dictate how we show up and how others perceive us. When we play small, downplay our accomplishments, and refuse compliments, we change the vibrations around us. When we are CONFIDENT in ourselves and our capabilities, we are rewarded with fulfillment, joy, and opportunities.

Think about the last time you interacted with a confident woman. Not an *arrogant* woman, a confident woman. A woman that knows she is perfectly flawed and perfectly capable of anything she sets her mind to. A woman who admires other women's success instead of comparing or judging. A woman who smiles and graciously accepts a compliment instead of playing it down. A woman who stands up for what is right and has finesse with her balance of assertion and empathy.

If we were in Vegas, I'd bet $100 that the confident woman encouraged you and elevated your confidence. She shined her light which allowed you to shine yours too. When we sit at the table with confident women, the conversation and vibration are simply different. It's positive, abundant, and energizing.

> **HERE'S A SECRET**
>
> *There is nothing more fierce than a confident & empowered woman.*
> _____

When we surround ourselves with doubters and negative people with low self-worth, we feel small too. The energy isn't abundant, and we feel insecure and timid.

How are you showing up? Are you a confident fountain of love and light, or are you a negative drain? As the saying goes, your vibe attracts your tribe.

There is nothing more fierce than a confident and empowered woman. **She knows there is enough success for ALL of us.**

You are perfectly flawed and 100% authentic. Be confident in THAT. You didn't come to be her; you came to be YOU.

Who you are is who you believe you are. Be bold. Be confident. Be YOU. Change the narrative in your head to confidence and abundance. Then show up as the perfectly flawed, confident woman you are.

"IT'S NOT WORKING OUT" IS WORKING OUT

If we can just let go and trust that things will work out the way they're supposed to, without trying to control the outcome, then we can begin to enjoy the moment more fully. The joy of the freedom it brings becomes more pleasurable than the experience itself.

GOLDIE HAWN

"IT'S NOT WORKING OUT" IS WORKING OUT

Every single thing that has happened in your life has gotten you to where you are today: the good, the bad, the victories, the lessons, and the mistakes. They've made you who you are.

When I was in my 20s, I was asked during an interview, "If you could change one thing from your life or one thing from history, what would you change?" I replied, "I'm a big believer in the butterfly effect. Everything that has happened—good, bad, or ugly—has shaped our reality. It made us who we are today. Rewriting and changing history seem a little frightening to me. So if I really had to change one thing, I guess I'd make it so Michael Jackson never got weird." *(Yeah, I got the job.)*

I believe the same thing about my life. As much as I'd love to go back and tweak or change a few things, I wouldn't. All of the decisions, circumstances, and life events have made me who I am. All the things that didn't work out somehow ended up working out.

I've finally figured out that I'm never going to figure it out. Right when you think you've mastered something, change occurs.

It's a curious thing—when things don't work out like we thought or planned, they ALWAYS end up working out.

Pastor Adam Hamilton, who founded the Church of the Resurrection in Leawood, Kansas, often reminds his congregation, "The worst thing is never the last thing." It's definitely a shining light of hope when you feel lost, defeated, or down on your luck.

Take a minute to think about something in your life that didn't work out the way you thought. At the time, you were devastated. You wondered how you'd ever move on or move through it. And then it ended up working itself out.

It's a curious thing. But I can't think of one time in my life that something not working out didn't end up working out.

Have you ever put a bid on a house that you LOVED, and then you didn't get it? Someone outbid you, the deal didn't go through, or some other freak thing got in the way, and you were incredibly bummed out. You thought it was the PERFECT house. You thought it was YOUR house. This has happened to Scott and me a few times.

One time, we stumbled upon a house we were extremely interested in even though we weren't even in the market for a house. But there was something about the house (it was like it was calling us). We toured the house and instantly fell in love. We thought it was meant to be. We thought it was meant to be our house.

Well, we didn't get the house; we were so disappointed that we were outbid. This house was supposed to be ours! In a last-ditch effort, we even wrote a letter to the homeowner telling them that if anything changed, we wanted the house and would even raise our offer. We never heard back from them.

It didn't work out.

But then we found another house! The house was listed the night before we left on a vacation to Mexico. We managed to get a tour of the house that night, and we were 100% IN LOVE. It was even better than the house we lost. It was everything we ever wanted (or so we thought). It was beautifully decorated. It was a private lot with a pool. It had amazing fixtures. It had that wow factor but was also incredibly cozy.

And it was meant to be (after all, we found this house the night before we left for vacation). A day later, we would have been out of the country and unable to tour it. Less than twelve hours before we left for Mexico, we put in an offer for over asking price and jet-setted out of the country. As the plane took off, I remember talking about how we were going to have so much to celebrate on our vacation.

Well, two days and multiple offers into our vacation, we lost the house. Someone outbid us with an all-cash offer. We were devastated. That was THE house for us.

It didn't work out.

I was so bummed over the loss of this house. I spent months that summer daydreaming about what it would have been like to entertain and have parties at the pool. I wanted that house to be our house. So you can imagine my surprise and delight when six months later, that house came back on the market.

We couldn't wait to tour it again. However, this time it was different. It wasn't beautifully decorated and cozy. In fact, it was empty. We spent hours walking through the house, and as much as we wanted to love it, it turned out we didn't love it anymore. Something just didn't feel right. We passed on putting in an offer.

It didn't work out.

Months went by. We closely watched the housing market, but rarely would a house catch our eye enough to set up a tour with our agent. One Saturday, I noticed a beautiful property that had an open house. This was always our favorite way to view a house as we didn't have to bother our agent and could leisurely tour the home. The pictures of this house were gorgeous. It was a bit out of our price range and bigger than we thought we wanted, but we decided, 'What the hell. It never hurts to check it out." So off we went to the open house.

The house was beautiful in person. It needed some updating, but we fell in love. Come to find out, this house was our DREAM HOUSE. I could see myself in the kitchen cooking, I could see how amazing a pool would look in the backyard. I could see us hosting parties and entertaining family and friends, and I knew exactly where I'd put the Christmas Tree.

We put in an offer that felt good to us (under the asking price). They say, "The third time's a charm," and WE GOT THE HOUSE.

IT WORKED OUT!

We thought nothing could EVER compare to the other houses we lost. At the time, the losses felt disappointing and defeating. But the truth was we just hadn't found the *right* house yet. By the other houses not working out, it ended up working out.

We're still living in this dream house: *our* dream house, and we LOVE it. I've lived in seven houses in my lifetime, and I love, love, love this house more than I've ever loved a house before.

So, next time the cards don't fall quite as you think they should, when something doesn't work out, or even if something you deemed as a "failure" is still stinging, just know that it will work out. As Pastor Adam says, "The worst thing is never the last thing." It will take as long as it takes to work out. But it will work out just like it's supposed to.

As I write this Secret, I sit in my office of the house our family has called home for the last two years. We've made memories here. We've laughed here. We've cried here. We've partied here. And now, we've written books here.

Mark my words: "It's not working out" is actually going to work out.

I believe this in my heart of hearts and want you to believe it in yours too: the best is yet to come—ALWAYS.

ON

PURPOSE

If you can't figure out your

purpose, figure out your passion.

For your passion will lead you right

into your purpose.

BISHOP T.D. JAKES

ON PURPOSE

What is your purpose? Most of us don't have a clear answer to that question. It's hard to name and identify our life purpose. And as we continue to grow, change, and evolve, I believe our purpose can CHANGE. In total transparency, my life purpose wasn't clear to me until after I turned 40. And I'm also sure my purpose will continue to evolve and elevate as I grow older.

The good news is if you're 20 and reading this, you don't have to wait until you're 40 to find your purpose. And if you're 60 and still contemplating purpose, ask yourself the following questions:

What work, relationships, and activities provide you the most fulfillment?

What is challenging, creates vulnerability, requires tenacity, pushes boundaries, ignites fear, creates happiness and success for YOU, and is fueled by courage, love, and passion?

Your passion might not be the easiest work, and it might not always make you happy. But it is deeply FULFILLING. Whatever you just answered to the questions above, THAT is where your purpose lives.

To make an impact in this world, you don't have to win a Nobel Peace Prize, start a company, or make millions. To make an impact, you need to be who you came to be. Just share your gifts and shine your light.

One of the things I've learned is that being intentional and present is a lot more rewarding than hustling 24/7. Yes, you have to put in the work to be successful in life. There is no easy street. But you don't have to exhaust yourself by working all the time.

Here's a permission slip: You don't need to hustle constantly to be successful and live your purpose.

For many of us, our purpose is to be a daughter, sister, mother, wife, and friend. Make and take time to nurture your relationships. At the end of your life, your relationships will be what matter most. Don't be afraid to take time off "work." News flash: the work will always be there. Slow down enough to:

Be present.
Be intentional.
Be kind.
Be tenacious.
Be forgiving.
Be patient.
Be you.

Be who you came to be.

"THE SECRET OF LIFE."

The secret of life

is enjoying the passage of time.

JAMES TAYLOR

"THE SECRET OF LIFE."

Music has always been a passion and purpose of mine. My Mom and Dad instilled a strong love and appreciation for music in my brothers and me beginning when we were little. I still remember our record player and the giant speakers that filled my childhood home with music which led to a lot of dancing and laughter.

This love and appreciation for music continued for my brothers and me through college. In fact, my oldest brother made it his life purpose and has been a music educator for over twenty years. I played in the High School Band and Orchestra, and for two years in college, I was a theatre and voice major. Today you'll just find me singing in the shower or dancing in the kitchen, but music continues to be a source of love and purpose in my life.

We always have music playing in our house—from hip hop to jazz to alternative rock to the best of the '80s and '90s. We love and appreciate so many different genres of music. At the top of my list of the best ways to spend a weekend will always be attending live concerts and music festivals.

One of my favorite things about music is how it connects us to our purpose. Music helps us connect our thoughts and emotions.

Music moves our bodies and souls. We can listen to a song and sing, dance, or cry. Often, it's as if the artist wrote the song just for YOU.

One of my all-time favorite songwriters and storytellers is James Taylor. I've had the good fortune to see him in concert six times. I know the lyrics to almost every one of his songs. One of my favorite songs of his is "The Secret O' Life." I love this song so much that I have the lyrics printed and framed in my office. It's a simple song that reminds us that the time is going to pass anyway, so we might as well enjoy it.

Just as James has sung this song to me countless times, now I'm telling you, the secret to life is enjoying the passing of time. The time is going to pass anyway, so you might as well go all-in on YOU. Be who YOU came to be. Just like musicians, your "music" isn't going to be for everyone. For some people, you're not going to be enough. For others, you'll be too much. It's okay. You didn't come to be them; you came to be YOU.

Who did you come to be? What do you want to do with the rest of your life? Maybe you have fifty more years on this beautiful earth or maybe just five more days. No one is promised tomorrow. Whatever it is you want to pursue and achieve—DO IT. I promise you'll never regret believing in yourself beyond reason. And for what it's worth, *I* believe in you enough for the both of us. That's why I wrote this book. My life purpose and wish are for you to "be who you came to be."

The last "Secret" of this book is a letter for anyone who is feeling lost or grieving. You might think it's a curious ending to round out a book on being who you came to be, but it's actually a blend of two pivotal moments that led me to write this book in the first place.

It starts with a moment from my sweet grandmother that changed my life, my family's life, and now has ripple effects in the lives of thousands of women I've gotten to know and do life with. And it continues in the aftermath of one of the most tragic events in my life: the unexpected passing of my father, which I wrote about earlier.

My secrets have highlighted the importance of pursuing your purpose every day. Even in your darkest days, YOU HAVE PURPOSE. And *that* reality alone makes this life worth living. The final Secret is for anyone and everyone who feels lost, is experiencing grief or has experienced grief.

> HERE'S A SECRET
>
> *Even in your darkest days, YOU HAVE PURPOSE. And that reality alone makes this life worth living.*

Grief is part of life. Grief is part of love.

I wrote this letter for myself, and I wrote this letter for YOU.

Never stop shining your light.

In your darkest days, your light can shine bright.

Be who you came to be.

A LETTER TO ANYONE
GRIEVING OR LOST

You don't know me, but I wanted to write you a letter—this final Secret—to tell you that you are loved.

I know things are dark right now. You feel lost, heartbroken and probably wonder if you will ever have genuine happiness again. The darkness might seem so heavy that you're finding it hard to shine your light. You might even wonder if you can shine your light.

I've been there. And I know how hard it is. Even the smallest daily routines can seem like climbing Mount Everest. Years ago, I lost my Dad unexpectedly, and it shattered me. It turned my world upside down and extinguished the daily joy and happiness in my life.

Just like you, I wondered, "Will my light ever shine again?"

I want you to know the answer is YES. YES, your light will shine again, and your light is STILL shining in the darkness.

Genuine happiness is in your future. But right now, you need to give yourself the space to work through whatever it is you're working through. It's part of the uplevel that *will* happen. Think of it like the caterpillar who goes into metamorphosis. It's a dark, slow, and "solo" journey. No one can help the caterpillar but the caterpillar itself. And then when it's READY, *and only when It's READY,* it emerges as a beautiful butterfly.

You will emerge.

I want you to know it's okay to feel lost. Oddly enough, feeling lost presents an opportunity to truly find ourselves. The saying is, "Be who you CAME to be." The path to discovery is messy and full of disruptions and uncertainty.

HERE'S A SECRET

I want you to know it's okay to feel lost. Oddly enough, feeling lost presents an opportunity to truly find ourselves.

You have so many gifts and authenticities. Right now, you are struggling, and it's OKAY. It's okay to struggle and feel "off." As I've said over and over . . . *you're only human.*

Give yourself space and permission to feel whatever it is you're feeling. Feeling it all is going to help you work through this tough time.

I don't know you, but I believe in you. I believe the universe works in magical ways. Most likely, we've never met. Maybe you found my book, and it intrigued you, or maybe someone gifted it to you. This book got in your hands, not by chance—it was meant to be.

My eighty-seven-year-old grandmother wrote a letter for my little boy before she died. She wrote a beautiful letter that was filled with sentiments on what he might be like, what his passions might be, what he will look like, and how she loved him deeply. But it was the last two sentences of her letter that took my breath away. The last two sentences she wrote were this:

"Be who you came to be. Love will guide you."

She could have written a lot of things. She might have offered advice to be tenacious, bold, kind, patient, courageous, or a leader. But she didn't. She wrote, "Be who you came to be." As if he was born predestined to do something amazing with his life.

I think my children were born predestined to do something amazing. I think I was born predestined to do something amazing, ***and I think YOU were born predestined to do something amazing with yours.***

She didn't write this letter just for Ben and Jack. She wrote it for me to share with the world, to share with people like YOU who are feeling lost and are unsure of the path and future.

I've never written a letter to a stranger before. But here I am, writing you this letter. Maybe it's my grandmother in heaven sending her message to YOU. That she wants you to "be who YOU came to be."

The last line of her letter was this: *"LOVE will guide you."*

If you are unsure of your path and what step to take next—let LOVE guide you. Embrace your passions, gifts, talents, light, and FAMILY. *That* is LOVE. **You are loved.**

You CAN find the courage, strength, and love to shine your beautiful light. Never give-up on you and who you came to be.

"Love. It's why we're all here." It was the toast my grandmother gave at our wedding, and there's no better or more simple Secret I could leave with you after all the words preceding this page.

"Love. It's why we're all here."

Most of the time, we just want to know we're not alone and that we are loved. You're not alone, you're never alone, and you are loved.

Thank you for reading my book. I'm passionate about sharing this message with the world. In my darkest days of personal grief and sadness, "be who you came to be" has been my North Star.

Now put down this book and go tell someone you love them. *"I love you"* is not a set of three words that you should ever "save." No one can ever be told they are loved "too much." And if you haven't heard it in a while, I want you to know that YOU are loved. I love you.

Love never runs out. Love never ends.

Be Who You Came to Be.

xoxo—Tara

IT'S

why

WE'RE

ALL

HERE

notes

1. We Are Social. "Digital 2021: The Latest Insights Into the "State of Digital" Simon Kemp. January 27, 2021. Retrieved from https://wearesocial.com/blog/2021/01/digital-2021-the-latest-insights-into-the-state-of-digital

2. American Psychological Association. "Odyssey's End: Lay Conceptions of Nostalgia Reflect Its Original Homeric Meaning." August 22, 2011. Erica G. Hepper, Constantine Sedikides, and Tim Wildschut, School of Psychology, University of Southampton, Southampton, UK; Timothy D.Ritchie, Department of Psychology, University of Limerick, Limerick, Ireland. Retrieved from http://www.southampton.ac.uk/~crsi/Hepper%20Ritchie%20Sedikides%20Wildschut%202012%20Lay%20conceptions%20of%20nostalgia.pdf

3. Johns Hopkins University. "Positive outlook linked to reduction in cardiac events." Stephanie Desmon. August 2013. Retrieved from https://hub.jhu.edu/gazette/2013/august/positive-outlook-cardio-health/

4. Blanchard, Kenneth H, and Spencer Johnson. *The One Minute Manager*, 1982. Print.

5. Blanchard, Kenneth H, and Spencer Johnson. *The One Minute Manager*, 1982. Print.